THE
CATHOLIC
IN
RECOVERY
Workbook

"Scott Weeman has beautifully fused the effectiveness of the Twelve Step recovery model and the wisdom of the Church into a compassionate, interactive guide. This workbook will make a difference in the lives of many faithful Catholics in recovery for years to come."

Rachael Killackey
Founder and executive director
Magdala Ministries

"Scott Weeman deftly handles one of the most complex subjects at the intersection of faith and real life: addiction. His personal, clinical, and ministerial experience shine through the pages of this workbook, which many will find helpful and potentially lifesaving. This is a gift to the Church."

Roy Petitfils
Licensed therapist and author of *Helping Teens with Stress, Anxiety, and Depression*

Praise from Catholic in Recovery Participants

"I have been delighted to see Catholic in Recovery grow in my parish, my community, and throughout the world. After several decades of recovery from compulsive overeating, it's refreshing to find a fellowship and a workbook that blends the sacraments with the Twelve Steps. What a gift to the Church!"

Sr. Margaret
Portland, Oregon

"Catholic in Recovery is the link I was missing in my more that twenty-year Al-Anon recovery program. *The Catholic in Recovery Workbook* uses scripture readings along with the Twelve Steps in a way that is relatable to my Catholic faith, bringing Jesus Christ and a loving God to the forefront of my program."

Diane
Panama City Beach, Florida

"Catholic in Recovery and *The Catholic in Recovery Workbook* have been amazing sources of strength for me. As a result of God's grace and working the Steps with a small CIR workbook group, my family relationships are healing and I've remained sober from alcohol, drugs, and lust for longer than I can ever remember."

John
Chula Vista, California

THE
CATHOLIC
IN
RECOVERY

Workbook

*A Guide to
The Twelve Steps*

Ave Maria Press   Notre Dame, Indiana

NIHIL OBSTAT
I have concluded that the materials presented in this work are free of doctrinal or moral errors.
Bernadeane M. Carr, STL
27 July 2022

IMPRIMATUR
+Ramon Bejanaro
Auxiliary Bishop
Diocese of San Diego
27 July 2022

Founded in 1865, Ave Maria Press is a ministry of the United States Province of Holy Cross.

www.avemariapress.com

Paperback: ISBN-13 978-1-64680-178-7

E-book: ISBN-13 978-1-64680-179-4

Cover and text design by Samantha Watson.

Printed and bound in the United States of America.

Library of Congress Cataloging-in-Publication Data is available.

CONTENTS

HOW TO USE THIS WORKBOOK

There is no one way to use this workbook, just as there is no one way to work a program of recovery. However, there are certain approaches to help you get the most out of it. To begin, this workbook was designed to be worked through with *at least one other person*. In other words, you should not use the workbook by yourself—this is especially true if you've never completed the Twelve Steps before. As St. Paul reminds us, "We must consider how to rouse one another to love and good works. We should not stay away from our assembly, as is the custom of some, but encourage one another" (Heb 10:24–25).

Following St. Paul's timeless wisdom, we *strongly* recommend using this workbook in collaboration with others, whether that's one-on-one with a sponsor, with a Catholic in Recovery group, or with some other recovery/Twelve Step group. This is important because so much of our recovery depends on the support, companionship, and encouragement of others. That's why throughout the workbook we stress the importance of working recovery alongside others, or "staying in the herd." The Recovery Team Roster in the back of the workbook (found on page 161) might help keep key members of your herd organized in one place.

One of the many reasons for staying in the herd is that we might not have much hope of finding recovery and healing when we first start working the Steps—that is to say, when we finally admit our powerlessness over addiction. Yet, when we begin this journey of recovery alongside others, we can borrow their hope until we're able to claim hope as our own.

A second important reason for using this workbook with others is that they can keep us accountable for completing the discussion questions, activities, and exercises. Remember, it's not enough to merely read this book. It's a *work*book, after all, and so it's designed to be worked through. We've found the best way to do this—and keep doing it—is alongside others. If you are interested in facilitating a small workbook group, see appendix IV on How to Facilitate a Small Workbook Group (found on page 175).

There will be portions of the workbook that you'll work through on your own, during which you'll reflectively and prayerfully complete various exercises, worksheets, and inventories. Space is provided at the end of each section for your work, although some exercises will require additional writing space. Certain activities, such as the Consequences Inventory, Resentment Inventory, Fear Inventory, and Sex and Finance Journal, may provoke sensitive responses that are best kept private. Therefore, you may choose to keep them in a separate journal or workspace. Upon completion of each exercise, you will be encouraged to discuss your progress with your sponsor, your small workbook group, and those in your Catholic in Recovery meetings.

You should use this workbook under the guidance of someone who has already worked the Twelve Steps, whether that's your sponsor or at least one other person in your small workbook group. While it's not necessary that they be familiar with this particular workbook, they should have worked through the traditional Twelve Steps of recovery.

This workbook is divided into four major parts, each aligning with a Catholic sacrament: I. Baptism, II. Reconciliation, III. The Eucharist, and IV. Confirmation. The Twelve Steps are featured in order individually over the course of these four parts. And within each Step, numbered sections explore particular themes. Each theme relates to recovery, the Catholic sacramental life, or both. It will be these individual sections that you'll work through one at a time—prayerfully reading the material, answering the discussion questions, completing the activities and exercises, and discussing your progress with a sponsor and / or your small workbook group.

In each of the twenty sections of the workbook, you will find these features:

- **Exploration and Understanding**. We'll explore each theme through the lens of recovery literature, scripture, the *Catechism of the Catholic Church*, testimonials, the wisdom of the saints and theologians, spiritual tools, and more for the purpose of coming to a fuller understanding of that theme and how to apply it to our recovery journey.
- **Reflection Questions**. We'll invite you to think about and respond to questions related to the section's theme. In addition to writing your answers down, you'll be encouraged to discuss them with your sponsor and / or small workbook group.
- **Prayer**. To conclude each section, we offer a helpful prayer from recovery or the Catholic tradition.
- **Putting the Steps into Action**. This is where the heart of recovery takes place. We'll work on a variety of exercises and activities to deepen and solidify what we've considered in the section. Similar to the reflection questions, you'll be encouraged to discuss your progress on these exercises and activities with your sponsor and / or small workbook group.

While the workbook follows the Steps in order, there is no specific timeline for completing it. Working the Steps can be quite challenging. As Jesus tells us, it's only by dying to our old and sinful selves—an often painful process—that we can bear fruit. That's why it's essential not to rush through the sections of this workbook. It might take one person a week or two to get through a section, while another person may need a month (or longer). It's not about getting to the end of a race or rushing through the Steps with the expectation that we'll magically be "recovered" by the end of them. As we'll explore throughout the workbook, working the Twelve Steps is a lifelong process and is never "finished."

With that said, there is also the danger of delaying our progress and, well, simply not doing the work required for each section at a reasonable pace. This is why it's so important, again, to use this workbook with your sponsor and / or a small workbook group. Others can hold us accountable when we make excuses or rationalize our lack of progress—both real temptations that can keep us floundering in our recovery.

Finally, our specific journey may look different from someone else's, depending on the addiction or unhealthy attachment with which we're struggling. As a result, there will be testimonials and recommendations in this workbook that may not appear to correspond to the specific addiction or unhealthy attachment that you need help with. While some nuance is needed when addressing different addictions, all addictions and unhealthy attachments point to a similar spiritual wound. They are merely different symptoms of the same spiritual sickness. Whether we're dealing with alcoholism, drug addiction, compulsive overeating or restricted eating, sex addiction and/or pornography, or a gambling problem, this workbook offers the Steps, insight, and practices that, when accepted and followed in collaboration with God's grace, can lead to our healing and recovery. In other words, the Twelve Steps coupled with the sacraments have the power to set us free no matter our particular struggles.

Ultimately, as long as we're doing our best, the success of our recovery depends on the merciful grace and love of Jesus Christ. That's why this workbook is grounded in developing a strong faith in Christ and his Church through the gift of the sacraments. No matter the depth and gravity of our addictions and unhealthy attachments, all things are possible for the One who loves us.

So, take heart and remember that you are infinitely loved by God! And with hope, let's begin our journey from the death of addiction to a new life of healing, grace, and love.

To accompany you through each section of *The Catholic in Recovery Workbook*, we have developed a digital platform with learning modules that include instructional and testimonial videos, printable worksheets, written content to supplement the workbook material, and a host of other addiction recovery tools that integrate Catholic spirituality. You can access this supplemental platform and find a small workbook group by visiting www.catholicinrecovery.com/cirworkbook.

Part I
BAPTISM

STEP 1

*We admitted we were powerless
over addictions, compulsions,
and unhealthy attachments —
that our lives had become
unmanageable.*

SECTION 1

SPIRITUAL PRINCIPLES

Many people, nonalcoholics, report that as a result of the practice of A.A.'s Twelve Steps, they have been able to meet other difficulties of life. They think that the Twelve Steps can mean more than sobriety for problem drinkers. They see in them a way to happy and effective living for many, alcoholic or not.

—*Twelve Steps and Twelve Traditions*, pp. 15–16

Exploration and Understanding

We now begin our journey through the Twelve Steps of recovery—a journey that has brought healing, transformation, and new life to countless people over many years. With God and others in recovery, we have so many reasons to be hopeful as we begin!

"Baptism" comes from the Greek word *baptizein*, which means "to plunge." When we are baptized in Christ, we are plunged into the living waters of renewal and healing. The *Catechism of the Catholic Church* tells us that our soul is marked indelibly through Baptism (1272) and that the Lord has claimed us as his own. We are given the grace to leave our old ways behind and live according to the Spirit as God's children.

Similarly, we are invited to "plunge" into the first Step of recovery, turning away from our addictive habits and unhealthy thinking patterns as well as our denial, shame, and fear. We take this plunge when we're ready to admit our powerlessness and our need for God.

Our transformation through recovery is a process that will require a willingness to be honest, the encouragement and hope of others, and, most importantly, a reliance on God's mercy. As we work the Steps, we'll also be adopting a new set of life principles. By "principles," we mean guidelines for conduct that do not change regardless of our circumstances or feelings.

Whether we know it or not, we all live by certain principles. The problem is that in the midst of our addiction our principles have been unhealthy, selfish, and contrary to our flourishing. For example, we may have been living by the principle that we deserve and need a drink after a long day of work. Or that we have to watch football on Sundays no matter what. Or that we can never trust another person because it's too risky.

3

The unhealthy principles we live by are often not consciously chosen but stem from sub-conscious habits and unreflective behaviors. Part of working the Steps entails uncovering these unhealthy principles and replacing them with healthy ones. It's important to remember that if we don't make an effort to identify and live intentionally by a set of principles, we end up adopting the principles of those around us—and those can be unhealthy and destructive.

So, what are some examples of healthy principles that we'll be adopting? There are many. Below are some principles that are necessary for working the Steps and finding healing in recovery.

- Honesty
- Faith
- Hope
- Courage
- Acceptance
- Willingness
- Humility
- Self-Discipline
- Confidentiality
- Perseverance
- Service
- Unity
- Trust
- Progress
- Fellowship
- Respect

There are some common misunderstandings about addiction recovery. Before we get too far, let's clarify a few things:

- Addiction does not discriminate.
- Addiction is not a moral referendum on one's life.
- No human power can relieve us of addiction.
- It is easier to put on slippers than to carpet the world.

There are a host of other concise phrases and slogans that capture key insights, which we'll explore in a future section. Similar to principles, these simple truth statements will be essential for us to adopt and internalize. They can help us move from delusional and false thinking to the healing light of truth and hope.

Barriers to Change

Despite our desire to begin recovery, there are many barriers to change that can make this journey a challenge. Denial, shame, fear, resentment, self-pity, selfishness, and pride are some of the potential obstacles that can keep us isolated within ourselves and unwilling to undergo the Steps to receive God's healing. Yet, the good news is that we can indeed overcome these obstacles by cooperating with God's grace—the grace that he deeply desires to pour over us!

In his book *Change or Die*, Alan Deutschman details the three phases required to undergo lasting change in our lives:

- *Relate*: Form a new, emotional relationship with a person or community that inspires and sustains hope.
- *Repeat*: Utilize this new relationship to learn, practice, and master the new habits and skills that we'll need.
- *Reframe*: Learn new ways of thinking about our situations and lives by means of this new relationship.

The steps above are exactly what recovery and the Twelve Steps are all about. We *relate* by joining a recovery community that offers us hope and encouragement on our journey. We *repeat* by walking alongside our sponsor and others in our recovery community to develop new habits as we work the Twelve Steps. And we *reframe* by gaining a new perspective on our thinking, enabling us to take responsibility and make meaningful and lasting changes in our lives. Deutschman highlights that this approach is proven to be much more effective than relying on the mistaken assumption that facts, fear, and force propel behavioral change, especially among those who are addicted.

When we are ready to admit that we are powerless over our addiction and that our lives have become unmanageable, we will grasp the importance of adopting new, healthy principles to guide our conduct.

Recovery Tool

Intentionally adopt for yourself a set of healthy principles to live by so that you can avoid living according to someone else's.

Reflection Questions

Take time to think about and write down responses to the following questions. Once you've done so, discuss your responses with your sponsor and/or small workbook group.

- How has denial, shame, or fear kept you isolated from God and away from seeking a spiritual solution?
- What has been your experience with the spiritual principles of the Twelve Steps and the Catholic Church?

Prayer

The Serenity Prayer

God,
Grant me the serenity
to accept the things I cannot change,
the courage to change the things I can,
and the wisdom to know the difference.

Living one day at a time,
enjoying one moment at a time,
accepting hardship as the pathway to peace.
Taking, as he did, this sinful world as it is,
not as I would have it.
Trusting that he will make all things right
if I surrender to his will.
That I may be reasonably happy in this life,
and supremely happy with him forever in the next.
Amen.

Putting the Steps into Action

This is where the real work of recovery takes place. Complete the following exercises before moving on to section 2:

- ☐ Spiritual Principles Worksheet
- ☐ Barriers to Change Worksheet
- ☐ Vision of Hope Inventory

Spiritual Principles Worksheet

1. What does the word "principle" mean to you?

   _____

   _____

2. What principles have you lived by throughout your life (spiritual or otherwise)?

   _____

   _____

   a. How have your actions reflected these principles?

   _____

   _____

   b. How have these principles served you and others?

   _____

   _____

   c. Which unhealthy principles are you willing to let go of?

   _____

   _____

3. What new spiritual principles are you seeking to adopt as you grow in your recovery journey? Explain.

   _____

   _____

4. What healthy new spiritual principles do you think will be the most challenging to adopt? Why?

   _____

   _____

Barriers to Change Worksheet

Denial

1. Describe a moment or moments in your life when you were unwilling to face the truth about your addiction/compulsion/unhealthy attachment.

_____

_____

    a. What impact did this have on you and others?

_____

_____

2. Are there people, places, or things you've avoided so as to not be reminded about your condition?

_____

_____

Shame

3. *Shame* is defined as "a painful feeling of humiliation or distress caused by the consciousness of wrong or foolish behavior." When have you felt ashamed about your addictive/compulsive behavior?

_____

_____

    a. How have these feelings shaped your personal identity and your relationships with others, God, and yourself?

_____

_____

Fear

4. How do you think fear impacts your health, wellness, and capacity to grow?

_____

_____

5. How might fear get in the way of your making progress through this spiritual work?

_____

_____

Vision of Hope Inventory

What are ten things you want out of a life that is free from your addiction, compulsion, or unhealthy attachment? Do not hesitate to dream big here!

1. _____

2. _____

3. _____

4 _____

5. _____

6. _____

7. _____

8. _____

9. _____

10. _____

SECTION 2

POWERLESSNESS

What else does this craving, and this helplessness, proclaim but that there was once in man a true happiness, of which all that now remains is the empty print and trace? This he tries in vain to fill with everything around him, seeking in things that are not there the help he cannot find in those that are, though none can help, since this infinite abyss can be filled only with an infinite and immutable object; in other words by God himself.

—Blaise Pascal

Exploration and Understanding

One of the hardest things about starting recovery is admitting we can't do it on our own— that we are powerless over preventing addiction from controlling our lives. After telling ourselves for so long that we are in control, despite everyone and everything around us indicating otherwise, we eventually accept that we are not. By the grace of God, we realize that the only way to freedom is by *embracing* our powerlessness.

This is what happened to Emily. She struggled with alcoholism for fifteen years, working hard to keep her addiction hidden from others. And after she became critically ill and was given medication to help manage her pain, it wasn't long before she was abusing the medication, too. Things only got worse from there. As she shares, "It just spiraled out of control, drinking around the clock, snorting pills, and manipulating doctors for more pills."

In other words, Emily had lost control of her life. She was utterly and completely powerless. Many of us know what it feels like to be at the mercy of our addictions, and to feel that, no matter what we say or do, we just can't break away from the awful cycle. Part of the reason this is so difficult is that addiction often takes root and manifests in four fundamental ways.

The Four Manifestations of Addiction

- *Biological*: Biological manifestations of addiction include the intense physical cravings not experienced by temperate users of a given substance (alcohol, drugs, food, etc.). These cravings can also affect participants in certain unhealthy behaviors (codependency,

11

gambling, pornography, etc.). As our tolerance for a substance or behavior grows, we require more and more of that substance or form of behavior to achieve the same level of stimulation.

- *Cognitive*: Cognitive manifestations of addiction often take the form of obsessive thoughts and unhealthy mental activities. We obsess about things related to our addiction (where or when we'll get our next high, our perceived "need" of a particular substance or behavior, etc.). As we read in *Twelve Steps and Twelve Traditions*, "we have warped our minds into such an obsession for destructive thinking that only an act of Providence can remove it from us" (p. 21).

- *Emotional*: Emotional manifestations of addiction cause a number of unhealthy and unpleasant feelings and attitudes. We become anxious, jittery, depressed, highly sensitive to both perceived and real slights and offenses, adopt a perpetual attitude of victimhood, and more.

- *Spiritual*: Spiritual manifestations of addiction include loneliness and a general sense of alienation from God. When we attempt to fill this God-shaped hole with unhealthy substances or behaviors, we only widen and deepen it. By fueling our addiction, we prevent ourselves from turning to the One who has the power to truly satisfy. As St. Augustine beautifully reminds us, "Our hearts were made for you, O Lord, and they are restless until they rest in you."

When we allow addiction to dominate our lives, we become powerless in the areas of our physical, mental, emotional, and spiritual health. As we'll see when we begin working on our Consequences Inventory at the conclusion of this section, the heart of the first Step is coming to terms with the biological, cognitive, emotional, and spiritual consequences of our behavior on ourselves and others. Without doing so, we remain unaware of just how pervasive, demanding, and harmful our addictions are.

This was no doubt the case for Emily. At one point, when she ended up in the ER due to her addictions, she received the Sacrament of the Anointing of the Sick. But even that wasn't enough to pull her out of this terrible cycle. She continued to drink and use drugs despite it nearly killing her.

Even though Emily no longer had power over her own life, all was not lost. After a particularly terrible outing of binge drinking, she stumbled into Mass the next morning. She was welcomed with loving arms by her parish community, and she started to realize what so many of us in addiction struggle to accept—we cannot save ourselves on our own. Soon after this, she admitted her need for God's help. "I got on my knees and prayed like I never have before. I truly believe I experienced a miracle that day," Emily said.

This is the Good News of the Gospel. Jesus Christ came to set captives free—to free us of our addictions and unhealthy attachments by his healing grace. And like Emily, we can take the first step to saying yes to God's offer of healing and freedom by admitting and embracing our powerlessness over our addiction.

> ### *Recovery Tool*
> **Stay in the herd by forming and maintaining a connection to a community in recovery and at your parish. By doing so, you will find the strength and support that, with the aid of the Holy Spirit, can help you find healing through recovery. In the back of this workbook, you'll find a template for creating your personal Recovery Team Roster.**

Reflection Questions

Take time to think about and write down responses to the following questions. Once you've done so, discuss your responses with your sponsor and/or small workbook group.

- How does your addiction manifest in each of the four areas detailed above (biological, cognitive, emotional, and spiritual)?
- What are some examples of your own powerlessness over addiction in your life?

Prayer

Prayer of St. Dominic

May God the Father who made us bless us.
May God the Son send his healing among us.
May God the Holy Spirit move within us and
give us eyes to see with, ears to hear with,
and hands that your work might be done.
May we walk and preach the word of God to all.
May the angel of peace watch over us and
lead us at last by God's grace to the kingdom.
Amen.

Putting the Steps into Action

This is where the real work of recovery takes place. Complete the following exercises before moving on to section 3:

☐ Consequences Inventory

☐ List of Yets

Be advised that the Consequences Inventory is vital to establish a foundation for your recovery, and we strongly encourage you to make time to complete it in a thoughtful and intentional manner.

Consequences Inventory

For many of us, addiction and compulsive behaviors build slowly over time, making it difficult to actually see how life has changed. Consequences that even a casual outside observer could readily identify as severe have gradually become the norm. Thus, the insanity of addiction looks perfectly ordinary to the addict. The same can be said of the behavior of an individual who attempts to control/hide/withdraw from the addiction of a spouse, child, parent, or other family member.

The easiest way to break through denial and fear is to create a list of consequences related to *your* behavior. In creating your Consequences Inventory, you should list as many items as possible, breaking them down into emotional, physical, spiritual, family and partnership, career and educational, and other consequences.

Emotional Consequences

These may include hopelessness, despair, guilt, shame, remorse, depression, paranoia, anxiety, loss of self-esteem, loneliness, emotional exhaustion, fear of going insane, feelings of internal conflict (living a double life), suicidal thoughts, homicidal thoughts, fear of the future, and more. List your emotional consequences below:

_____

_____

_____

_____

_____

_____

_____

Physical Consequences

These may include high blood pressure, weight loss, weight gain, trouble sleeping or waking up, physical exhaustion, sexually transmitted diseases, attempted suicide, and more. List your physical consequences below:

_____

_____

_____

_____

_____

_____

Spiritual Consequences

These may include feelings of disconnection, abandonment, anger toward God, or emptiness; loss of faith, of values and morals, or of interest in the well-being of others; missing Mass; and more. List your spiritual consequences below:

_____

_____

_____

_____

_____

_____

Family and Partnership Consequences

These may include damaged romantic relationships, loss of respect, alienation from family members, being disowned, threatened or actual loss of spouse or partner, threatened or actual loss of parental rights, jeopardizing of your family's well-being, and more. List your family and partnership consequences below:

_____

_____

_____

_____

_____

_____

Career and Educational Consequences

These may include diminished performance, demotion, underemployment, loss of respect from coworkers, acting out at work, poor grades or job reviews, not getting promoted, getting fired or dismissed from school, losing a chance to work in one's career of choice, and more. List your career and educational consequences below:

_____

_____

_____

_____

_____

_____

Other Consequences

These may include loss of interest in formerly enjoyable activities, lack of self-care, loss of important friendships, loss of community standing, financial problems, involvement in illegal activities, near arrests, arrests, legal issues, incarceration, and more. List your other consequences below:

_____

_____

_____

_____

_____

_____

_____

List of Yets

While progressing through the Consequences Inventory, we might hear others share about consequences they've faced that have not happened to us. Not *yet*, that is. For whatever reason (perhaps we just simply haven't been caught, yet), we have not lost everything and may still hold on to a few things of value. If you are beginning your recovery and find yourself thinking that there are still more possible consequences if nothing changes, it is wise to list them here:

_____

_____

_____

_____

_____

_____

_____

_____

_____

_____

_____

_____

_____

_____

_____

SECTION 3

UNMANAGEABLE

> Those who are well do not need a physician, but the sick do. I did not come to call the righteous but sinners.
>
> —Mark 2:17

Exploration and Understanding

We see over and over again in the gospels that Jesus aligns himself with the spiritually sick—sinners in need of God's saving grace and mercy. He eats with tax collectors and prostitutes. He seeks the lost sheep of Israel. And he does so not to judge or condemn them, but to love and forgive them. A critical moment for our recovery is accepting that our lives have become unmanageable—that we are sick and in need of a savior.

For years, Jim struggled with an addiction to pornography and masturbation. Not only did this strain his marriage tremendously, but it got so bad that he was fired from his job for viewing pornography at work and lost his social work license. Despite his efforts to stop, which included attending counseling sessions with his wife, completing pornography recovery courses, and reading various books on the topic, he could not escape the scourge of his addiction. Put simply, his life had become *unmanageable*.

Perhaps you are in this position right now. Perhaps, after years of trying to stop on your own—of trying to manage your addiction without the help of others—you still feel trapped, spiraling, and sick.

The good news is that by accepting that our lives have become unmanageable, we open ourselves up to God's grace. It's only when we admit that our lives are out of control that Jesus, the divine physician, can sit at the table of our heart and heal us.

But this is hard, and, unfortunately, many refuse to admit that their lives have become unmanageable. As we read in *Alcoholics Anonymous*, there are those who "by every form of self-deception and experimentation . . . try to prove themselves exceptions to the rule" (p. 31).

If we are unwilling to admit we are sick, then we won't ask for healing. Instead, we'll likely keep looking for other sources to blame for our illness—our family and friends, upbringing and childhood, environment and circumstances, even God. This is why sometimes hitting rock bottom is necessary because at that moment we are faced with a reality we cannot deny. We realize we are unable to save ourselves.

Jim hit rock bottom when he lost his job. Fortunately, he continued to seek God's healing and eventually completed a self-directed retreat outlined in Fr. Michael E. Gaitley's *33 Days to Merciful Love: A Do-It-Yourself Retreat in Preparation for Consecration to Divine Mercy*. While Jim didn't have any reason to believe this particular attempt at healing might be different from any of his previous ones, he felt compelled to give it a try.

Something miraculous happened. After decades of failing to free himself from his addiction to pornography and masturbation, he received the grace to finally overcome it through Jesus's offer of divine mercy. It was through admitting that his life was unmanageable and turning to Christ's mercy that Jim was able to receive the healing and freedom he had desired for so long.

As he explains, "The keys to victory are growing to trust in God's love, mercy, and sufficiency, regular immersion in God's Word, fellowship in community, the wonderful sacraments of the Eucharist and Reconciliation, and, lastly, God's amazing grace!"

In the sacramental life of the Church, Baptism opens us up to God's loving and healing touch, making us his sons and daughters. As the *Catechism of the Catholic Church* explains, "Immersion in water symbolizes not only death and purification, but also regeneration and renewal" (1262). This is similar to what happens when we open ourselves up to God from the depths of our addiction. While painful, this opening up allows us to die to the sinful, addicted self and make way for the renewal of the Holy Spirit.

The spiritual truth of renewal through Baptism is noted by St. Paul, who tells us that "we were indeed buried with him through baptism into death, so that, just as Christ was raised from the dead by the glory of the Father, we too might live in newness of life. For if we have grown into union with him through a death like his, we shall also be united with him in the resurrection" (Rom 6:4–5).

When we admit our powerlessness over our addiction, we undergo the painful process of being submerged in the healing waters of God's love, much like Baptism. We die to self so as to live anew in Christ. Like Jim, we too can surface to the healing touch of God's amazing grace.

Recovery Tool
When we blame others instead of accepting responsibility for our addictions, we only hurt ourselves and stall our recovery.

Reflection Questions

Take time to think about and write down responses to the following questions. Once you've done so, discuss your responses with your sponsor and/or small workbook group.

- How do you understand your baptism through the lens of powerlessness and unmanageability?
- What previous attempts have you made to manage your life and your addiction?

Prayer

Prayer from *The Twelve Steps and the Sacraments*

Lord,
I begin this process seeking an open heart and an open mind.
Please help me shed my personal ambitions
for the sake of finding a new experience with you.
Please enable me to set aside everything I think I know
for an open mind and a new experience.
Remove any denial that may get in the way
of seeing my condition exactly as it is.
Help me to see the truth about addiction
and the parts of my life that shut out the sunlight of the Spirit.
Offer me the opportunity to see the true meaning
of powerlessness over people, places, and things.
Just as your own baptism identified you with the broken
and made you one with sinners,
I look to the waters of baptism to acknowledge my broken ways
and clothe myself in your redeeming grace.
Thank you for providing me this path
to co-creating my life with you, my blessed Lord.
Amen.

Putting the Steps into Action

This is where the real work of recovery takes place. Complete the following exercises before moving on to section 4:

☐ Unmanageability Journal

☐ Baptism Reflection

Immerse yourself in the Word of God by reading chapter 6 of St. Paul's Letter to the Romans, exploring the fullness of the Sacrament of Baptism.

Unmanageability Journal

> **Step 1:** We admitted we were powerless over addictions, compulsions, and unhealthy attachments—that our lives had become unmanageable.

Reflect and journal about how your life has become unmanageable.

1. What does it mean to you to manage your life?

_____

_____

_____

2. What have you done in the past to manage your life in response to your addiction, compulsion, or unhealthy attachment (or the addiction of a loved one)?

_____

_____

_____

3. What is it like for you to admit that your life has become unmanageable?

_____

_____

_____

4. In what ways has your understanding of powerlessness and unmanageability changed?

_____

_____

_____

Baptism Reflection

> Baptism is God's most beautiful and magnificent gift. . . . We call it gift, grace, anointing, enlightenment, garment of immortality, bath of rebirth, seal, and most precious gift. It is called gift because it is conferred on those who bring nothing of their own; grace since it is given even to the guilty; Baptism because sin is buried in the water; anointing for it is priestly and royal as are those who are anointed; enlightenment because it radiates lights; clothing since it veils our shame; bath because it washes; and seal as it is our guard and the sign of God's lordship.
>
> —St. Gregory the Theologian

Spend time reflecting on each of these components of our baptism, putting your understanding of the Sacrament of Baptism in your own words and incorporating the wisdom of the *Catechism of the Catholic Church* (1213–1284).

Gift:

_____

_____

_____

Grace:

_____

_____

_____

Anointing:

_____

_____

_____

Enlightenment:

_____

_____

_____

Garment of Immortality:

_____

_____

_____

Bath of Rebirth:

_____

_____

_____

Seal:

_____

_____

_____

STEP 2

Came to believe that a Power greater than ourselves could restore us to sanity.

SECTION 4

CAME TO BELIEVE

When anyone places his whole trust in God, hoping in and serving him faithfully at the same time, God watches over him, to the extent of his confidence, in every danger.

—St. Francis de Sales

Exploration and Understanding

What does it mean to believe that God can save us? While it includes an intellectual assent to God's existence, *belief* for the Christian goes much further. It means trusting that nothing is impossible for God—that he alone can restore us to sanity, give us new life, and rescue us from the darkness of addiction.

Kathy spent decades denying she had a problem with drugs and alcohol. She was raised Catholic but drifted away from the Church as an adolescent, heading down a path of self-sufficiency. She turned to sex, parties, drugs, and alcohol, and before she graduated from high school she had had two abortions. The guilt she felt from her abortions only made things worse. "I spiraled out of control, using anything to numb the pain, shame, and regret from what I had done," Kathy said. Her life continued this way as she entered adulthood, got married, and had children. Throughout it all she remained far from God.

Coming to believe that God can save us is a necessary part of recovery. But for so long we have let our self-will run riot. We have grasped at the illusion of self-sufficiency, raising many obstacles to being dependent on God. In fact, for some of us raised in the Church, it can be even more difficult to give our lives over to God because the idea of God and religion may carry with it all sorts of baggage.

As *Twelve Steps and Twelve Traditions* explains, "Sometimes [recovery] comes harder to those who have lost or rejected faith than to those who never had any faith at all, for they think they have tried faith and found it wanting. They have tried the way of faith and the way of no faith. Since both ways have proved bitterly disappointing, they have concluded there is no place whatever for them to go" (p. 28).

Below are five reasons why we might struggle to find—or reclaim—faith in God.

Five Reasons for Weakened Faith

- *Indifference*: By allowing the lures of the world to entice us, we can become indifferent to God. There are many things we can allow to occupy our minds and hearts, such as worldly success, pleasure, power, entertainment, and so on. If we are not intentional about fostering our faith, we become indifferent to God.
  - "The great danger in today's world, pervaded as it is by consumerism, is the desolation and anguish born of a complacent yet covetous heart, the feverish pursuit of frivolous pleasures, and a blunted conscience. Whenever our interior life becomes caught up in its own interests and concerns, there is no longer room for others, no place for the poor. God's voice is no longer heard, the quiet joy of his love is no longer felt, and the desire to do good fades." —St. Maximilian Kolbe

- *Self-Sufficiency*: In our culture, self-sufficiency is often seen as a virtue. While it's noble to take responsibility for our lives and act accordingly, an excessive focus on being independent can lead us to believe we don't need God, or anyone else.
  - "If you are discouraged it is a sign of pride because it shows you trust in your own power. Your self-sufficiency, your selfishness, and your intellectual pride will inhibit his coming to live in your heart because God cannot fill what is already full." —St. Teresa of Calcutta

- *Prejudice against Religion*: It isn't hard to see the mistakes, failings, and sins of those involved in organized religion, including the Catholic Church. And we can rightly be hurt and angered by the sinfulness we witness. But if we allow these feelings to fester in unhealthy ways, we may end up with an unreflective prejudice against religion that keeps us from God.
  - "We, who have traveled this dubious path, beg you to lay aside prejudice, even against organized religion. We have learned that whatever the human frailties of various faiths may be, those faiths have given purpose and direction to millions. . . . We missed the reality and the beauty of the forest because we were diverted by the ugliness of some of its trees. We never gave the spiritual side of life a fair hearing." —*Alcoholics Anonymous*, pp. 49–50

- *Defiance*: We can turn our backs on God when our lives haven't worked out the way we've hoped or planned. Our dreams may never have come to fruition. Certain relationships may remain broken. We may have suffered terrible tragedies. So, to get back at God, we turn from him in defiance.
  - "So it's not strange that lots of us have had our day at defying God himself. Sometimes it's because God has not delivered us the good things of life which we specified. . . . More often, though, we had met up with some major calamity, and to our way of thinking lost out because God deserted us. At no time had we asked what God's will

was for us; instead, *we* had been telling him what it ought to be." —*Twelve Steps and Twelve Traditions*, p. 31

- *Scrupulosity*: Scrupulosity is an obsessive concern with one's own sins and compulsive performance of religious devotion. It can stem from an obsessive reliance on controlling our relationship with God. It's about following all of the rules and reciting the "right" words rather than personally connecting with God. It is discipline without trust. The problem is that this type of relationship with God does not allow the space for faith and humility. It demands control over God. And as our efforts for control become fruitless over time, we may turn toward despair, resentment, and addictive behavior.
  - "He believes he is devout. His religious observance is scrupulous. He's sure he still believes in God, but suspects that God doesn't believe in him. . . . Valiantly he tries to fight alcohol, imploring God's help, but the help doesn't come." —*Twelve Steps and Twelve Traditions*, p. 32

There are other barriers that keep us from believing in God or having strong faith, but the above five are some of the most common. In each case, we do not humbly seek God's mercy. Instead, we cling to a superficial understanding of God and the spiritual life, not having made an honest inventory of our moral faults, sought to make amends with those we've harmed, freely given to others without expecting anything in return, and prayed as often as we can "Thy will"—and not our own—be done.

Kathy had tried to achieve sobriety—had even attended Twelve Step meetings—but continued to relapse. It was the loss of her grandchild that finally brought her to God and, eventually, sobriety.

"I became sober in order to help comfort my daughter through the pain and sorrow of losing a child, and it was during that time that I came to believe that as long as I stayed close to God, I would never use again," Kathy said. She was forced to ask herself three questions: Who is this God whom I must now trust and rely upon? How do I find him? And why would he forgive me, a sinner?

Tragedy stirred her to authentic faith in God, and she became sober on June 1, 2006. Two years later, she received the Sacrament of Confirmation at the Easter Vigil, completing her initiation into the Catholic Church and returning to her childhood faith with joy. Afterward, while on a spiritual pilgrimage to Bosnia and Herzegovina, she received profound healing in the Sacrament of Reconciliation for her two abortions.

Put simply, Kathy came to believe in and experience God's healing and merciful touch. The good news? So can we.

> ### Recovery Tool
> **Trusting God doesn't mean bringing our plans to God and asking him to bless them. It means asking God to open our eyes to his plans for our lives and to give us the grace to embrace them.**

> ### Recovery Tool
> **God moves mountains—but he asks us to pick up the shovel.**

Reflection Questions

Take time to think about and write down responses to the following questions. Once you've done so, discuss your responses with your sponsor and / or small workbook group.

- Consider the five reasons for weakened faith—indifference, self-sufficiency, prejudice against religion, defiance, and scrupulosity. Which ones apply most to you? Explain.
- What do you fear losing by becoming dependent on God? What holds you back from believing he can truly help you?

Prayer

The St. Anselm Prayer

O Lord my God,
Teach my heart this day where and how to see you,
where and how to find you.
You have made me and remade me,
and you have bestowed on me all the good things I possess,
and still I do not know you.
I have not yet done that for which I was made.
Teach me to seek you, for I cannot seek you unless you teach me,
or find you unless you show yourself to me.
Let me seek you in my desire,
let me desire you in my seeking.
Let me find you by loving you,
let me love you when I find you.
Amen.

Putting the Steps into Action

This is where the real work of recovery takes place. Complete the following exercises before moving on to section 5:

☐ Barriers to Belief Journal

☐ Share your work from Step 1 (Vision of Hope Inventory, Consequences Inventory, List of Yets, Unmanageability Journal, and Baptism Reflection) with your sponsor and/or small workbook group

 Hearing how others have overcome various barriers to belief can be beneficial as we approach our own barriers. Visit the digital platform at catholicinrecovery.com/cirworkbook for video testimonies on how others have approached Step 2 and to access supplemental workbook materials.

> Sometimes [recovery] comes harder to those who have lost or rejected faith than to those who never had any faith at all, for they think they have tried faith and found it wanting. They have tried the way of faith and the way of no faith. Since both ways have proved bitterly disappointing, they have concluded there is no place whatever for them to go. The roadblocks of indifference, fancied self-prejudice, and defiance often prove more solid and formidable for these people than any erected by the unconvinced agnostic or even the militant atheist.
>
> —*Twelve Steps and Twelve Traditions*, p. 28

Consider the five reasons for weakened faith (indifference, self-sufficiency, prejudice against religion, defiance, and scrupulosity) and describe how you relate to each. What patterns and actions in your life help overcome each obstacle?

Indifference

> Whenever our interior life becomes caught up in its own interests and concerns, there is no longer room for others, no place for the poor. God's voice is no longer heard, the quiet joy of his love is no longer felt, and the desire to do good fades.
>
> —St. Maximilian Kolbe

How I relate:

_____

_____

_____

Patterns and actions that help overcome:

_____

_____

_____

Self-Sufficiency

If you are discouraged it is a sign of pride because it shows you trust in your own power. Your self-sufficiency, your selfishness, and your intellectual pride will inhibit his coming to live in your heart because God cannot fill what is already full.

—St. Teresa of Calcutta

How I relate:

_____

_____

_____

Patterns and actions that help overcome:

_____

_____

_____

Prejudice against Religion

We used to amuse ourselves by cynically dissecting spiritual beliefs and practices when we might have observed that many spiritually-minded persons of all races, colors, and creeds were demonstrating a degree of stability, happiness and usefulness which we should have sought ourselves.

—Alcoholics Anonymous, p. 49

How I relate:

_____

_____

_____

Patterns and actions that help overcome:

_____

_____

_____

Defiance

> At no time had we asked what God's will was for us; instead, we had been telling him what it ought to be. No man, we saw, could believe in God and defy him, too. Belief meant reliance, not defiance.
>
> —*Twelve Steps and Twelve Traditions*, p. 31

How I relate:

_____

_____

_____

Patterns and actions that help overcome:

_____

_____

_____

Scrupulosity

> He believes he is devout. His religious observance is scrupulous. He's sure he still believes in God, but suspects that God doesn't believe in him. He takes pledges and more pledges. Following each, he not only drinks again, but acts worse than the last time. Valiantly he tries to fight alcohol, imploring God's help, but the help doesn't come.
>
> —*Twelve Steps and Twelve Traditions*, p. 32

How I relate:

_____

_____

_____

Patterns and actions that help overcome:

_____

_____

_____

SECTION 5

RESTORE US TO SANITY

On the evening of that first day of the week, when the doors were locked, where the disciples were, for fear of the Jews, Jesus came and stood in their midst and said to them, "Peace be with you." When he had said this, he showed them his hands and his side. The disciples rejoiced when they saw the Lord. He said to them again, "Peace be with you. As the Father has sent me, so I send you." And when he had said this, he breathed on them and said to them, "Receive the holy Spirit."

—John 20:19–22

Exploration and Understanding

God is the one who can heal us and make us whole. He alone has the power to restore us to sanity. But if we need him to restore us to sanity—and we do—then it's worth exploring what we mean by *insanity*. Below are just a few ways we've perhaps let insanity reign in our lives:

- We continue doing the same thing over and over again and expect different results. "As dogs return to their vomit, so fools repeat their folly" (Prv 26:11).
- We refuse to accept that addiction is the disease that makes us believe we don't have a disease.
- We turn back to our addiction again and again because we fail to recall, thanks to our "built-in forgetter," the inevitable damage it causes to ourselves and others. (This is why, in Twelve Step groups, we encourage newcomers to share, because they keep us from forgetting about the pain and destruction of addictive behavior.)
- We engage in "euphoric recall," remembering only the good times from our addictive past and not the bad times.

In other words, being in a state of insanity allows our addiction to run rampant in our lives. It's living in a state of brokenness and sin. Yet, God desires us to be whole and holy, which is why he made us his children through Baptism and continues to extend grace to us through the other sacraments. Through grace he makes us new, rescuing us from insanity and sinfulness and restoring us to sanity and holiness.

"I had always had the feeling of being unlovable, even though I came from a loving family. I was adopted, and I wondered why my biological mother surrendered me. That got into my psyche. I felt that I had to earn my lovability," Stephanie said.

This feeling of having to earn love caused Stephanie to become a people pleaser, overly controlling, and to develop an eating disorder. Anorexia and bulimia would plague her for many years.

"Restricting your eating can feel powerful, but nothing can be more powerless. I had no life in me. Plus, since I was anorexic, I was like the walking dead," Stephanie said.

Stephanie sought secular therapy for many years to help manage her eating disorder, and while she developed helpful tools, she never experienced the freedom and healing for which she yearned. "Secular therapy never worked because I had a spiritual malady. The core problem was that I didn't believe I was lovable," she shared.

Although she was active in her Catholic faith, Stephanie struggled to see herself as a beloved child of God. Eventually, she realized she was alienating people on a regular basis and that she needed to get control of her eating disorder since it was continuing to bring destruction and unhappiness into her life. She looked for help online with the following three search terms: *addiction*, *Catholic*, and *powerlessness*. By God's grace, Stephanie found Catholic in Recovery.

"I went to a Catholic in Recovery meeting the next day. I was full of shame and fear, but I was curious because all of the people there seemed happy. I wondered how they could be happy and comfortable with who they are. How could they forgive themselves for all of the things they shared? It seemed to be proof to me that I could be happy again and forgive myself, but I just didn't know how," Stephanie said.

She continued to attend meetings and started working the Steps. One night she encountered Jesus in a miraculous way. "I was sitting on my sofa since I couldn't sleep, and I was having that feeling of unlovability. I then saw my son's graduation picture with his loving eyes, and I felt God reveal to me that this is how he sees me. I just stared at that picture and then told Jesus, 'I surrender to your love, and I'm going to let go and invite you in.' And it was like Jesus was sitting at the other end of the sofa, and when I said that—and I had never had an experience like this—he immediately took me into his arms and hugged me. I just started sobbing because I had never rested in Jesus's arms like that," Stephanie said.

The *Catechism of the Catholic Church* teaches us that "Baptism seals the Christian with the indelible spiritual mark (character) of his belonging to Christ. No sin can erase this mark, even if sin prevents Baptism from bearing the fruits of salvation. Given once for all, Baptism cannot be repeated" (1272). What good news this is! It means that despite our addiction, brokenness, sinfulness, and moments of insanity, we remain God's by virtue of our Baptism. *Nothing* we do can remove this indelible mark that sets us apart as one of God's beloved children. It's a gift freely given to us by God.

The *Catechism* expounds upon the sanctifying grace offered to us through Baptism. This grace:

- [Enables us] to believe in God, to hope in him, and to love him through the theological virtues;
- [Gives us] the power to live and act under the prompting of the Holy Spirit through the gifts of the Holy Spirit;
- [Allows us] to grow in goodness through the moral virtues. (1266)

In addition to receiving the grace to grow in holiness and wholeness, through Baptism we also become part of the Body of Christ and "individually parts of one another" (Rom 12:5). As the *Catechism* beautifully explains, our baptism "constitutes the sacramental bond of unity existing among all who through it are reborn" (1271).

This is important, because it means that being restored to sanity will come about through being part of Christ's Body, the Church. In other words, the success of our recovery depends on being in communion with others journeying toward Christ. *Alcoholics Anonymous* hits on this same truth, explaining that connecting with others who have "shared in a common peril" of addiction and are working to find God's healing is absolutely required (p. 17).

As Stephanie continued in her recovery, she came to see that only God—not herself or anyone else—could restore her to sanity. "My second Step was hard because I was still trying to restore myself to sanity through my own efforts and thinking. But I just begged God to help me turn myself over to him. And through the sacraments, through daily reception of the Eucharist, through adoration, and Reconciliation, I asked him to help me in my unbelief and he did," she said. "What I had been seeking with food, withholding it and overdoing it, was the infinite from the finite. And what is a sacrament if not the infinite in the finite? The Holy Spirit showed me that what I have been seeking I already have: God's unconditional love and forgiveness."

Through Catholic in Recovery meetings, the sacraments, and the Steps, Stephanie continues to discover just how beloved she is by God. "Attending Catholic in Recovery meetings was the first time I felt emotionally safe in a community. I had never had that and it was so healing and liberating. I could see changes in people, and they told me they could see changes in me. Over the course of time I saw the life of Christ rising up in others, and I witnessed healing, joy, and freedom in both my life and their lives," Stephanie said.

It's by seeing others who have been restored to sanity that we come to believe we too can be restored. We realize that God can do for us what we cannot do for ourselves. In community, we hear about others' weaknesses and wounds, the ones that God has transformed for his purposes yet still remain, which empower and encourage us in our recovery and spiritual journey.

But being in communion with others requires that we too are vulnerable with others. When we lead with our weaknesses, we find unity with others. And in unity we achieve victory.

WEAKNESS → UNITY → VICTORY

Jesus established a connection between vulnerability and unity when he appeared to the apostles after his Death and Resurrection. He showed them his wounds—the result of his taking on our sins and brokenness—but then offered them peace: "The disciples rejoiced when they saw the Lord. He said to them again, 'Peace be with you. As the Father has sent me, so I send you.' And when he had said this, he breathed on them and said to them, 'Receive the holy Spirit. Whose sins you forgive are forgiven them, and whose sins you retain are retained'" (Jn 20:20–23).

Jesus greets us as he greeted the apostles, by offering us peace and breathing the Holy Spirit on us. He says to us, "Shalom," which is a Hebrew blessing of wholeness and restoration.

When he visited them again the following week, Jesus invited Thomas to actually place his fingers in his wounded side and hands, to personally connect with Christ's suffering. By touching Jesus's wounds, Thomas was enabled to embrace the reality of his new, risen life (Jn 20:27). When we reveal our own wounds to others as they reveal theirs, we are connected to one another. We touch each others' lives and are united in our suffering as well as our hope. From this unity as members of the Body of Christ, we welcome God's Spirit of healing, peace, and comfort. Through our shared witness, together we come to believe that God can truly restore us to sanity.

Recovery Tool

It can be helpful to think of those helping us with our recovery and faith journey as members of our spiritual board of directors. These are people such as our sponsors, spiritual directors, priests, members of our Twelve Step meetings, and others. If you don't already have something like a board of directors, begin forming one. Then, once you have it in place, make sure to consult with its members regularly and often.

Recovery Tool

We must always remain in the hands of the divine physician, Jesus.

Reflection Questions

Take time to think about and write down responses to the following questions. Once you've done so, discuss your responses with your sponsor and/or small workbook group.

- What are some of the repeated, insane behaviors that keep you from finding union with the Lord?
- What actions can you take to believe that God can restore you to wholeness?

Prayer

Prayer from *The Twelve Steps and the Sacraments*

Lord,
Thank you for the moments
that have brought me to this place in my journey.
As I struggle to overcome the insanity, which can be overwhelming,
I place my faith in you as my Higher Power.
I ask for your protection and care as I take this step toward new life.
Great are the plans that you hold for me,
and I begin to grow in willingness to see those plans unfold.
Amen.

Putting the Steps into Action

This is where the real work of recovery takes place. Complete the following exercise before moving on to section 6:

☐ Cycle of Insanity Worksheet

 Commit to attending one or two additional recovery meetings this week, either a Catholic in Recovery meeting or another type of meeting specific to your experience with addiction. Remember from the section titled How to Use This Workbook that this process will be most beneficial if done in collaboration with others.

Cycle of Insanity Worksheet

Step 2: Came to believe that a Power greater than ourselves could restore us to sanity.

The wording of Step 2 implies an admission of our own insanity, which requires that we've properly worked through Step 1. Many have defined insanity as "doing the same thing over and over again and expecting different results."

1. How do you define and understand insanity?

   _____

   _____

   _____

2. Write about the behaviors that prove insanity as it relates to your addiction, compulsion, attachment, or response to a loved one's addiction (use extra space as necessary):

   _____

   _____

   _____

3. In what ways are you still practicing self-sufficiency in your daily life?

   _____

   _____

   _____

4. "As dogs return to their vomit, so fools repeat their folly" (Prv 26:11). Make a list of moments when you've returned to old behaviors (control, dishonesty, acting out) under the belief that you've been "cured" of the consequences.

   _____

   _____

   _____

5. Make a list of moments when God has given you a chance at redemption, describing how he has previously restored you to wholeness.

_____

_____

_____

STEP 3

*Made a decision to turn our will
and our lives
over to the care of God as we
understood Him.*

SECTION 6

SURRENDER

Practicing Step Three is like the opening of a door which to all appearances is still closed and locked. All we need is a key, and the decision to swing the door open. There is only one key, and it is called willingness. Once unlocked by willingness, the door opens almost by itself, and looking through it, we shall see a pathway beside which is an inscription. It reads: This is the way to a faith that works.

—*Twelve Steps and Twelve Traditions*, p. 34

Exploration and Understanding

Patrick started drinking in the 1960s and did so for nearly fifty years. While there were stretches when he didn't drink, sooner or later he always picked up the bottle again. Despite his drinking, he raised a family, owned multiple homes, and enjoyed a successful military and teaching career. Because the outward appearances of his life looked good, he didn't think he had a problem. And if he didn't appear to have a problem, then why turn his will and life over to the care of God?

What can make Step 3 so hard is that often we don't really believe we need to turn our will and life over to God. We think we can manage on our own just fine, ignoring the trail of destruction in our wake. This can especially be the case if we're good at making our outward appearance nice and polished, hiding what's really going on underneath. That is why hitting the proverbial rock bottom can be so necessary. Sometimes, that's the only thing that will force us to let go of the illusion that we can save ourselves.

In Patrick's case, he had to hit rock bottom. One night, after he received bad news, he began drinking. And he didn't stop. "I was drinking heavily and decided to go downstairs to get more alcohol. I ended up going head first. It was a serious fall, and I separated my shoulder," he shared. He could have easily been killed. Instead, it was a fall into grace, one that Patrick accepted. The night of his brutal fall down the stairs would be the last night he had a drink.

Even when we are convinced that only God can save us from our addiction, handing over our will and life is challenging. As we read in *Twelve Steps and Twelve Traditions*, Step 3 "looks hard, even impossible. No matter how much one wishes to try, exactly how can he turn his will and his own life over to the care of whatever God he thinks there is?" (p. 35).

Being part of a recovery community, staying within the herd, is vital for our success in this effort. It's by realizing that others have completed this seemingly impossible Step that we find the strength to do so ourselves. It's God who ultimately helps us work this Step, like all of the Steps. He only asks that we place the key of willingness into the lock of the door to freedom. As long as we crack the door with our own efforts, God can blow the door off of its hinges.

When this happens, we begin the process of breaking free from a cycle of spiritual shame and negative thinking. This thinking may not be conscious, but it nevertheless has been responsible for many of our feelings, behaviors, and motivations.

Thinking from a Cycle of Spiritual Shame

- "I am unlovable."
- "If people really knew me, they would reject me."
- "I can't count on anyone, including God, to meet my needs."
- "I need to find something that I can control that will meet my needs."
- "_____ is my greatest need and source of comfort."

Skewed shame is one of the rotten fruits of concupiscence. Thinking from spiritual shame is similar to thinking from concupiscence, which is our inclination to sin due to our fallen nature.

Thinking from Concupiscence

- "Just one more time."
- "Everyone else is doing it."
- "I'll get back on track tomorrow."
- "I won't get caught."

By turning our will and life over to God, we allow him to free us from these unhealthy thinking patterns, replacing the cycle of spiritual shame with a cycle of spiritual recovery.

Thinking from a Cycle of Spiritual Recovery

- "I am lovable."
- "If people really knew me, they could love me more."
- "I can count on others and God to meet my needs."
- "God and healthy relationships are my greatest need and source of comfort."

But how can we foster this type of healthy thinking? In other words, what exactly does giving our will and life over to God look like? It entails integrating principles of right conduct, disciplining our actions, building good habits by cooperating with God's grace, and serving others with generosity. This is what working the Steps is all about—cooperating with God's grace, one day at a time, to take responsibility for our actions, put our house in order, and love others as Christ does. This is what we mean by "the way to a faith that works" (*Twelve Steps and Twelve Traditions*, p. 34).

"All of the Twelve Steps require sustained and personal exertion to conform to their principles and so, we trust, to God's will. It is when we try to make our will conform with God's that we begin to use it rightly" (*Twelve Steps and Twelve Traditions*, p. 40). As we work the Steps, our self-centeredness and all of its rotten fruits—selfishness, pride, fear, self-pity, and so on—give way to the fruits of God's grace. They give way to works of corporal and spiritual mercy, which free us from the bondage to self that is the core malady affecting us all.

Corporal Works of Mercy	Spiritual Works of Mercy
• Feed the hungry	• Counsel the doubtful
• Give drink to the thirsty	• Instruct the ignorant
• Shelter the homeless	• Admonish the sinner
• Visit the sick	• Comfort the sorrowful
• Visit the imprisoned	• Forgive injuries
• Bury the dead	• Bear wrongs patiently
• Give alms to the poor	• Pray for the living and the dead

As we work the Steps, we are empowered by God's grace to be more merciful toward our neighbor and to escape the bondage of selfishness.

That night Patrick drunkenly fell down the stairs was the night the Lord broke into his life, inviting him to put away his addictive, destructive behaviors. But it was only the beginning of his journey of recovery—of working the Steps and adopting principles of right conduct. As Patrick worked the Steps in recovery, he started to become aware of the damaging effects of his behavior over the last several decades, especially of his failures as a husband and father. He also began attending Mass or a recovery meeting every day of the week. He committed to doing the Steps. He gave his will and life over to God.

"We alcoholic Catholics ain't gonna be able to turn our will over to God by just saying it," Patrick shared. "We gotta live it and think about it, and so the investment of our time in the faith is crucial."

Recovery Tool

We hand our will and life over to God by doing the work and working the Steps with the aid of God's grace. The best way to tell if someone has worked the Third Step is that they are working the Fourth Step.

Reflection Questions

Take time to think about and write down responses to the following questions. Once you've done so, discuss your responses with your sponsor and/or small workbook group.

- What does it mean to turn your will and life over to the care of God?
- Reflect on and share a moment when the "key of willingness" opened a locked door for you.
- How do you understand the saying, "This is the way to a faith that works"?
- How do merciful actions toward others relieve you of bondage to self?

Prayer

Third Step Prayer from *Alcoholics Anonymous*

God, I offer myself to thee
to build with me and to do with me as thou wilt.
Relieve me of the bondage of self, that I may better do thy will.
Take away my difficulties, that victory over them may bear witness
to those I would help of thy Power, thy Love, and thy Way of life.
May I do thy will always!
Amen.

Putting the Steps into Action

This is where the real work of recovery takes place. Complete the following before moving on to section 7:

☐ Memorize the Third Step Prayer

☐ Reverently recite the Third Step Prayer with your sponsor and/or small workbook group

 Give yourself permission to make a big deal about the ritual of surrendering through the Third Step Prayer, finding a quiet place that you can return to in the future to remember and rededicate yourself to recovery. You may also invite your spouse, family members, or other important people to join you.

Part II
RECONCILIATION

STEP 4

Made a searching and fearless moral inventory of ourselves.

SECTION 7

RESENTMENT INVENTORY

All bitterness, fury, anger, shouting, and reviling must be removed from you, along with all malice. [And] be kind to one another, compassionate, forgiving one another as God has forgiven you in Christ.
—Ephesians 4:31–32

Exploration and Understanding

A necessary component of our recovery is conducting a searching and fearless moral inventory. We'll work through different types of moral inventories over these next few sections, beginning with the Resentment Inventory. It's vital that we do this—that we turn up the stone of our souls so that God can remove the resentment festering there. This is no easy task, and one that certainly requires courage (after all, we're conducting a *fearless* moral inventory). However, when we complete Step 4 with the help of a sponsor and God's grace, the freedom we begin to experience is incredible.

Resentment is a sickness that keeps us from experiencing joy, healing, and happiness. In *Alcoholics Anonymous*, we read that "a life which includes deep resentment leads only to futility and unhappiness . . . this business of resentment is infinitely grave. We found that it is fatal. For when harboring such feelings we shut ourselves off from the sunlight of the Spirit" (p. 66).

God has given us desires that we're invited to fulfill in healthy ways. Our desires for material comfort, food, sex, pleasure, emotional stability, security, companionship, and so on are all good in and of themselves. They are meant to guide us toward human fulfillment and happiness—imperfect happiness in this life and perfect happiness in the next.

Yet, as we know only too well, problems arise when we allow these desires to run rampant. We might define addiction as an obsessive need to fulfill our desires beyond reason and at the expense of others' and our own well-being. As *Twelve Steps and Twelve Traditions* details with respect to the addict, "our desire for sex, for material and emotional security, and for an important place in society often tyrannize us" (p. 42).

When we desire and pursue such things inordinately, we sin. Our desire for companionship turns into the manipulation and use of others. Our desire for sex transforms into an obsession with pornography and masturbation. Our desire for pleasure leads to alcohol and drug abuse.

Of course, as we pursue these unchecked and self-serving desires, we'll inevitably hit obstacles. Other people, organizations, or circumstances will hinder or prevent us from fulfilling them. And we become angry when others do not accommodate our desires or when they try to stop us. We grow enraged when our efforts to satisfy our desires are curbed by other forces. The problem is that we have become so singularly focused on fulfilling our desires that whether such obstacles are actually *just and legitimate* doesn't matter. We're angry simply because our desires have been thwarted.

Resentment blocks the "sunlight of the Spirit," which is why St. Paul admonishes us not to let its scourge take root in our hearts: "Be angry but do not sin; do not let the sun set on your anger, and do not leave room for the devil. . . . All bitterness, fury, anger, shouting, and reviling must be removed from you, along with all malice. [And] be kind to one another, compassionate, forgiving one another as God has forgiven you in Christ" (Eph 4:26, 31–32).

St. Paul's language is explicit: by allowing resentment to fester, we leave room for the devil. As disciples of Christ, we are called to forgive as he has forgiven us. The path for both the Christian life and recovery requires acknowledgment of our shortcomings and forgiveness. We must forgive others and ourselves, as well as seek forgiveness from others. It's in Step 4 that we begin the difficult but grace-filled work of doing so.

Experience with the Sacrament of Reconciliation can be useful as we courageously begin this work. There are few other encounters available in this world which offer a glimpse of God's great mercy and love for us than what we find in the confessional. Recalling past experiences with God's mercy can propel us to honestly face the things we've long ignored—the things that have long influenced our behavior and capacity to return God's love to others.

To let go of our resentments, we have to be clear on what they are in the first place. It's amazing how many resentments we can find lurking within us once we take the time to examine and write them down. By bringing them to light, we allow Christ to heal us of our spiritual sickness: "From [resentments] stem all forms of spiritual disease, for we have been not only mentally and physically ill, we have been spiritually sick. When the spiritual malady is overcome, we straighten out mentally and physically. In dealing with resentments, we set them on paper. We listed people, institutions or principles with whom we were angry" (*Alcoholics Anonymous*, p. 64).

We now turn to conducting a Resentment Inventory. First, it's important to understand that this process isn't about identifying people or organizations that have harmed us just to justify our anger toward them. What we'll find is that when we take an honest inventory, we discover that many of our resentments are unjustified or the result of our own sin (or, at the very least, that we are partially to blame). For example, we may resent our spouse for their unwillingness to trust us and for treating us with suspicion. Yet, when we dig deeper, we may discover that our spouse is justified in having this attitude because of our consistently untrustworthy behaviors and habits.

Further, when we acquaint ourselves with our own moral shortcomings, we are better able to see others' moral shortcomings with compassion and humility. As St. Gregory the Great notes, the "consideration of our own faults will lead us to excuse those of others. For a person who piously considers that he also has something which others must bear patiently in him will be easily disposed to bear patiently injuries he receives from others."

Below are instructions on how to complete a Resentment Inventory. While we provide a Resentment Inventory exercise at the end of this section (page 56), you can simply create a table with four columns and as many rows as needed to account for each resentment.

The Four Columns of a Resentment Inventory

1st Column: *I resent*

- List a person, place, thing, institution, or principle (rule or expectation to live by) that you harbor resentment toward. List as many as you can (you may want to include yourself if you are regularly angry at yourself as well).
- Example: John Smith, Jane Johnson, Wisconsin State University

2nd Column: *Because*

- Describe the reason for your resentment. For each person, institution, or principle, there may be more than one cause of resentment. If so, list each cause in its own row (take as many rows as you need). Be as specific as you can. There is no shame in admitting your resentments, and you will only be sharing this inventory with a trusted individual.
- Example (for "John Smith"): John Smith told my girlfriend about my addiction and dishonesty. He took and sold a valuable item of mine because I hadn't paid him for rent. He has a better life than I do.

3rd Column: *Affects my*

- Detail how the resentment affects you. In other words, list whether it violates your self-esteem, security (physical, emotional, or financial), ambitions, personal relationships, and so on. This helps us understand how we feel threatened as well as gives us the opportunity to take a more objective look at our situation.
- Example (for "John Smith"): Self-esteem, Romantic relationship, Financial security, Ambitions

4th Column: *My part*

- This is the most crucial column of the Resentment Inventory, in which we admit our role in the resentment. We consider how we have been selfish, dishonest, afraid, prideful, or in denial. Although we may recognize that the circumstances around the resentment are not entirely our doing, in this column we are only focusing on our specific responsibility.

- Example (for "John Smith"): I was dishonest and prioritized addiction over relationships. I did not pay my portion of the rent to him. I've stolen from him. My feelings toward him reflect my own lack of esteem, and I am making prideful comparisons.

Finally, it's important to highlight some warnings before you begin working on your Resentment Inventory. Below are pitfalls to be aware of that can hinder, or even work against, completion of Step 4.

- Those with depressive tendencies may experience feelings of excessive shame and guilt when putting an inventory together. Be mindful of "reverse pride," which entails morbidly reflecting on past behaviors and future hopes.
- Those who are naturally self-righteous and grandiose will often consider this an unnecessary and offensive exercise. Failure to complete the inventory, however, will make it challenging to find joy, serenity, and peace, and likely only further old and destructive patterns.
- Some may be unwilling to complete the inventory until others in their lives make changes. Those having this attitude would be wise to shift the power they give to others to God and move forward with their inventory instead of waiting for something beyond their control.

Although taking this inventory can be a difficult and uncomfortable process, based on the feedback of countless individuals who have completed Step 4, we can say with confidence that the freedom, hope, and grace that come with completing it are astonishing. As always, the Lord will help us to make a searching and fearless moral inventory of ourselves if we only ask him and do our best to try.

Recovery Tool
The best way to gain esteem is by doing estimable things.

Recovery Tool
God gives us the grace to deal with what we need to deal with today, today.

Reflection Questions

Take time to think about and write down responses to the following questions. Once you've done so, discuss your responses with your sponsor and/or small workbook group.

- How have resentments kept you from living a peaceful, sober, and joyful life?
- What challenges stand in the way of recognizing your part in the fourth column of the Resentment Inventory?
- If you have completed a Fourth Step (and Fifth Step), please share about your experience and offer hope to those who have not yet done so.

Prayer

Prayer to St. Michael the Archangel

St. Michael the Archangel, defend us in battle.
Be our defense against the wickedness and snares of the devil.
May God rebuke him, we humbly pray,
and do thou, O Prince of the heavenly hosts,
by the power of God, thrust into hell Satan,
and all the evil spirits, who prowl about the world
seeking the ruin of souls.
Amen.

Putting the Steps into Action

This is where the real work of recovery takes place. Complete the following exercise before moving on to section 8:

☐ Resentment Inventory

 Similar to the Consequences Inventory in section 2, this will be a thorough process. It is important to be persistent through this stage of the Twelve Steps and to check in with your sponsor and/or small workbook group for motivation and support.

Resentment Inventory

Begin your Resentment Inventory by listing the people, institutions, and principles (rules or expectations to live by) that you resent in the first column. Then, describe the reason for your resentment in the second column. If there is more than one reason for a resentment, list each reason separately. For each cause of resentment, note how you are affected in the third column. It might be that your self-esteem, security (including physical, emotional, or financial security), ambitions, or personal relationships are threatened. Finally, and most importantly, conclude the fourth column by noting *your part* in the resentment and/or how your actions have furthered the resentment. In this column we express how we have been selfish, dishonest, afraid, prideful, or in denial. Although we recognize that the circumstances around the resentment were not all our doing, we only focus on our own part in the fourth column.

Sample Resentment Inventory

I resent	Because	Affects my	My part
John Smith	He told my girlfriend about my addiction and dishonesty.	Self-esteem; relationships	I was dishonest and prioritized addiction over relationships.
John Smith	He took and sold a valuable item of mine.	Security (financial); ambitions	I did not pay my portion of rent; I've stolen from him.
John Smith	He has a better life than I do.	Self-esteem	My feelings toward him reflect my own lack of esteem; making comparisons; prideful.

My Resentment Inventory

I resent	Because	Affects my	My part

SECTION 8

FEAR INVENTORY

What really hurts is not so much suffering itself as the fear of suffering. If welcomed trustingly and peacefully, suffering makes us grow. It matures and trains us, purifies us, teaches us to love unselfishly, makes us poor in heart, humble, gentle, and compassionate toward our neighbor. Fear of suffering, on the other hand, hardens us in self-protective, defensive attitudes, and often leads us to make irrational choices with disastrous consequences.

—Jacques Philippe, *Interior Freedom*

Exploration and Understanding

Fear can be a debilitating and pervasive emotion in our lives. It can keep us in the throes of addiction to alcohol, drugs, food, sex, gambling, or something else. As *Twelve Steps and Twelve Traditions* explains, "Unreasonable fear that our instincts will not be satisfied drives us to covet the possessions of others, to lust for sex and power, to become angry when our instinctive demands are threatened, to be envious when the ambitions of others seem to be realized while ours are not. We eat, drink, and grab for more of everything than we need, fearing we shall never have enough" (pp. 48–49).

Fear thrusts us into a never-ending cycle of destruction. Of course, it's reasonable and healthy to have a certain degree of fear in our lives, since fear can help us avoid danger. We should fear drinking again or losing ourselves to sexual immorality, for instance, because such things would derail our happiness and growth toward God. What we are concerned with here is the type of fear that runs rampant, controlling us, causing us to hurt others and ourselves, and keeping us from receiving the mercy of God.

Our Catholic tradition has much to say about fear as an obstacle in the spiritual life. St. Thomas Aquinas explains that "fear is such a powerful emotion for humans that when we allow it to take us over, it drives compassion right out of our hearts." St. Thérèse of Lisieux encourages us to raise our souls "to God by the elevator of love and not climb the rough stairway of fear." And St. Padre Pio exhorts us to "stop entertaining those vain fears. Remember it is not feeling which constitutes guilt but the consent to such feelings."

As we begin working through our Fear Inventory, similar to our Resentment Inventory, we'll examine each one of our fears—where it comes from, how it affects us, and our part in it.

This is challenging. And as we embark on a searching and fearless moral inventory, we will likely experience, well, fear. As we read in *Twelve Steps and Twelve Traditions*, "it must seem to every newcomer that more is being asked of him than he can do. Both his pride and his fear beat him back every time he tries to look within himself. Pride says, 'You need not pass this way,' and Fear says, 'You dare not look!'" (p. 49).

It takes courage to honestly face, assess, and take responsibility for our fears, which is why we do not do it alone but with Christ, our sponsor, and others in recovery. It's a process that is never finished; for this reason, in recovery circles you'll often hear the phrase "progress, not perfection." Similar to our resentments, our fears can be numerous and deeply rooted, so it is essential we conduct a Fear Inventory as part of our larger moral inventory.

Even though this isn't easy, we should not be afraid! We find in scripture over and over again the exhortation to not be afraid. In Christ, we overcome fear with love.

As we'll discover, many of our fears indicate a desire for control—a tendency to be overly self-reliant. This keeps us from humbly accepting how dependent we are on God. Even when we feel confident, cocky, and bold, often these attitudes merely mask insecurities and fear of failure. A fear that others might realize we've been "faking it" the whole time. That we're not the person we desperately want others to believe we are and, therefore, are unlovable.

After relying on ourselves for so long, with little success, it can be hard to submit ourselves to God's care. But it's by acknowledging our fears that we're able to hand them over to God and ask him to remove them (as only he can). "We trust infinite God rather than our finite selves. We are in the world to play the role he assigns. Just to the extent that we do as we think he would have us, and humbly rely on him, does he enable us to match calamity with serenity" (*Alcoholics Anonymous*, p. 68).

Below are instructions on how to complete a Fear Inventory. While we provide a Fear Inventory exercise at the end of this section (page 64), you can simply create a table with four columns and as many rows as needed to account for each fear.

The Four Columns of a Fear Inventory

1st Column: *I fear:*
Here are a few questions to consider as you're listing your fears:

- Does fear about my ability as a(n) (employer/parent/spouse/provider) disrupt my confidence and ability to be present?
- Are there disappointments or traumas from the past that I try to avoid at all cost?
- What (perceived) violations of truth, beauty, and goodness am I afraid may be exposed to others?
- Do I fear being "found out" about something?

- Is there something I fear will happen to me or others? Examples: *My kids being exposed to my addiction; Rejection by loved ones; Conflict with others*

2nd Column: *Because:*
The second column allows us to describe the nature of the fear and invites us to reflect on why this fear exists. Here are a few questions to consider:

- Am I acting in a way that I should not be acting?
- Do I fear that some secret of mine will expose me negatively?
- Is there an unhealthy principle I'm living by that might be violated?
- Example (for "Conflict with others"): *I have rarely been exposed to healthy conflict; my parents were manipulative and dishonest. I feel at fault when others are uncomfortable. I feel shame and anxiety that I am at fault.*

3rd Column: *Affects my:*
This part of the Fear Inventory helps us understand how our instincts might be threatened when dealing with each fear. You can classify the parts of "self" affected by social instincts, security instincts, love/sex instincts, and ambition:

- **Social instincts**: personal relationships, pride, self-esteem, prestige, companionship
- **Security instincts**: material, emotional
- **Love/Sex instincts**: acceptable love/sex relationships, hidden love/sex relationships
- **Ambitions:** security, social, romantic
- Example (for "I have rarely been exposed to healthy conflict; my parents were manipulative and dishonest"): *Personal relationships; Social ambitions; Emotional security instincts*

4th Column: *My part:*
In the fourth column, we attempt to identify the exact nature of our wrongs. Here are a few questions to consider:

- Do I try to overcome feelings of fear and insecurity by lying, cheating, manipulating, hiding the truth, or acting out in my addiction/compulsion?
- Does my pride keep me from being honest and acting with integrity?
- Do I gossip with others to undercut those with whom I compare myself?
- In the case of [a particular fear], what did I do initially to get the ball rolling?
- How could I have done things differently?
- Example (for "I have rarely been exposed to healthy conflict; my parents were manipulative and dishonest"): *I fail to speak up and have not had an adult conversation with my parents about this.*

Even after we do a thorough inventory, new resentments and fears will surface. Once again we'll need to admit them, take responsibility for them, and bring them to the light of Christ's healing touch. In fact, this is exactly what we're called to with the Sacrament of

Reconciliation. Exposure to our fears, resentments, and shortcomings can produce shame if we are distant from God and the sacraments. However, with God's aid, we can delight in such awareness knowing that his grace awaits us in Confession.

It can be frightening to conduct a Fear Inventory, but by doing so under the guidance of an experienced sponsor and with the grace of God, we can take the next Step. And as we'll discover, the more Steps we take, the easier they become. "As we persist, a brand-new kind of confidence is born, and the sense of relief at finally facing ourselves is indescribable. These are the first fruits of Step 4" (*Twelve Steps and Twelve Traditions*, pp. 49–50).

Recovery Tool

Comparing our "insides" to other people's "outsides" is a recipe for resentment, jealousy, and self-pity.

Recovery Tool

Don't leave before the miracle happens. And don't leave after it happens, either.

Reflection Questions

Take time to think about and write down responses to the following questions. Once you've done so, discuss your responses with your sponsor and/or small workbook group.

- How would you describe your experience of working through the Fourth Step so far?
- Share two or three fears that come to mind when brainstorming what you will include in column one of the Fear Inventory. Explain why you have the fear, how it affects you, and your part in the fear.

Prayer
Hail Holy Queen

Hail, holy Queen, mother of Mercy,
our life, our sweetness, and our hope.
To thee do we cry,
poor banished children of Eve;
to thee do we send up our sighs,
mourning and weeping

in this valley of tears.
Turn then, most gracious advocate,
thine eyes of mercy toward us;
and after this our exile, show unto us
the blessed fruit of thy womb, Jesus.
O clement, O loving,
O sweet virgin Mary.
Amen.

Putting the Steps into Action

This is where the real work of recovery takes place. Complete the following exercise before moving on to section 9:

☐ Fear Inventory

 Listen to others as they express an understanding of their own fears, either in your workbook group discussions, at meetings, or in one-on-one conversations if the topic comes up. Sometimes exposure to another's self-awareness can clue us in to an understanding of ourselves.

Fear Inventory

Begin your Fear Inventory by listing each of your fears in the first column. Then describe the cause of your fear in the second column, adding any details that will be helpful for self-reflection. If there is more than one cause for a fear, note it in a separate row. Then, for each cause, describe how you are affected in the third column. It might be that your social instincts (personal relationships, pride, self-esteem, prestige, or companionship), security instincts (material or emotional), love/sex instincts (acceptable or hidden), or ambitions (security, social, or romantic ambitions) are threatened.

Finally, and most importantly, conclude the fourth column by noting *your part* in the fear. Did you attempt to overcome feelings of fear and insecurity by lying, cheating, manipulating, hiding the truth, or acting out in your addiction/compulsion? Did your pride keep you from being honest and acting with integrity? Did you gossip with others to undercut those with whom you compare yourself? What did you do initially to get the ball rolling? How could you have done things differently? Provide a thorough inventory of your fears, and spend time speaking with others who have completed a Fear Inventory to help uncover fears you may not be able to recognize.

Sample Fear Inventory

My Fear Inventory

I fear	Because	Affects my	My part
Conflict	I have never been exposed to healthy conflict; parents were manipulative and dishonest.	Personal relationships; social ambitions; emotional security instincts	I fail to speak up and have not had an adult conversation with my parents about this. Failure to forgive.
Conflict	I feel at fault when others are uncomfortable.	Self-esteem; pride; personal relationships	Valuing others' approval over God's; needing to be liked by others
Conflict	Shame and anxiety that I am at fault.	Security ambitions; emotional instincts; self-esteem	Sometimes I am at fault; expectations of perfection; disconnection from God

My Fear Inventory

I fear	Because	Affects my	My part

SECTION 9

SEXUAL AND FINANCIAL CONDUCT

Sin creates a proclivity to sin; it engenders vice by repetition of the same acts. . . . Vices can be classified according to the virtues they oppose, or also be linked to the capital sins which Christian experience has distinguished, following St. John Cassian and St. Gregory the Great. They are called "capital" because they engender other sins, other vices. They are pride, avarice (greed), envy, wrath, lust, gluttony, and sloth or acedia.

—*Catechism of the Catholic Church, 1865–1866*

Exploration and Understanding

We will now turn to the final activity of Step 4: examining our sexual and financial conduct. It's important that we look at these two aspects of our lives—specifically, at how they have manifested in sinful, unhealthy, and harmful ways. Inordinate behaviors in the areas of sex and finance often stem from the same source—an inability to delay gratification and a desire for immediate pleasure on our terms. St. Thomas Aquinas teaches that we are tempted to seek pleasure, power, honor, and wealth in an effort to fulfill our deepest desires that only God can fulfill. This can manifest in our lives through poor decisions around money and sexual relationships.

These are areas of concern even if we do not individually struggle with an addiction or unhealthy attachment related to sex (such as pornography, masturbation, etc.) and/or finances (such as gambling, compulsive debting, etc.). If we examine our conduct in these areas, we may find that our addiction or unhealthy attachment in another area has negatively effected them as a consequence. Hopefully we've learned by now that addiction is never an isolated aspect of our lives—its destructive tentacles stretch over the whole of our own and our loved ones' lives. By honestly looking at how we have failed in these two areas, we put ourselves in a position to make appropriate amends to those whom we've hurt, later in our recovery.

The good news is that when we do the difficult work of unearthing our faults and sins, we allow the merciful gaze of Jesus to fall upon them and us. The goal of conducting a searching and fearless inventory is never to simply uproot our sins and leave them exposed. Rather, we lay them bare to invite Christ into our lives to forgive and heal us. We acknowledge them so that after experiencing the healing grace of Christ—most concretely and efficaciously in the Sacrament of Reconciliation—we can draw upon this grace to uproot sin and amend our lives.

The questions below will help us examine our sexual and financial conduct. You can also find these questions in the Sex and Finance Journal on page 73 at the end of this section.

Keep in mind that a healthy integration of our sexual lives is a vital part of the recovery process, as evidenced by many saints and the direction of the Twelve Steps. We do not disdain the body or scorn the desire for sexual intimacy when rightly ordered. We must review our sexual conduct in order to find the freedom to truly love others. This is a process we continue throughout our recovery and spiritual development.

Questions for examining our sexual conduct:

- How has my pursuit of sexual relations damaged others, put others in harm's way, or destroyed my sense of self?
- Who would be hurt if they knew of any sexual behavior I do in secret?
- How have others and I been impacted by my unhealthy pursuit of sexual pleasure? How did I react when confronted?
- Have I demanded sexual arousal from others?

Questions for examining our financial conduct:

- Have I been honest with my spouse regarding my financial behavior?
- Have I stolen from others or been paid for work that I have not honestly completed?
- Have I borrowed money recklessly without considering the impact of not paying the money back?
- Do I live above my means, borrowing money or going into debt to support an unreasonable lifestyle?
- Which of the seven deadly sins (listed later in this section) have contributed to my financial instability? Explain.
- When have I been dishonest about my financial behavior?

Before examining our sexual and financial conduct and thus completing the final piece of our searching and fearless moral inventory, let's consider sin as a whole—and what we can do to combat it with virtue steeped in God's grace. Over the centuries, the Church has taught that all of our sins stem from seven capital vices, also called the seven deadly sins:

> Sin creates a proclivity to sin; it engenders vice by repetition of the same acts. This results in perverse inclinations which cloud conscience and corrupt the concrete

judgment of good and evil. Thus sin tends to reproduce itself and reinforce itself, but it cannot destroy the moral sense at its root. Vices can be classified according to the virtues they oppose, or also be linked to the capital sins which Christian experience has distinguished, following St. John Cassian and St. Gregory the Great. They are called "capital" because they engender other sins, other vices. They are pride, avarice (greed), envy, wrath, lust, gluttony, and sloth or acedia. (*Catechism of the Catholic Church*, 1865–1866)

The good news is that by cooperating with the grace of God we can overcome our proclivities to sin—our vices—with virtue and love. Below we've detailed each of the seven capital vices, or sins, paired with the corresponding virtues that we should strive to cultivate instead.

Pride vs. Humility

Pride is having an overly high opinion of oneself; exaggerated self-esteem; conceit, arrogance, vanity, self-satisfaction. It is foundational to many other sins and unhealthy attachments. In Matthew's gospel, Jesus provides clear guidance about avoiding unhealthy pride: "Take care not to perform righteous deeds in order that people may see them; otherwise, you will have no recompense from your heavenly Father. When you give alms, do not blow a trumpet before you, as the hypocrites do in the synagogues and in the streets to win the praise of others. Amen, I say to you, they have received their reward" (Mt 6:1–2).

Humility, on the other hand, is the acknowledgment that God is the author of all good. Humility avoids inordinate ambition or pride and provides the basis for turning to God in prayer. It is wise to remind ourselves frequently of the familiar adage, "There is a God—and it's not me."

Humility is fostered by acts of service to others and gratitude toward God; it is essential to recovery. "Blessed are the poor in spirit, for theirs is the kingdom of heaven" (Mt 5:3).

Greed vs. Generosity

Greed is an excessive desire for acquiring or having more than one needs or deserves. Sometimes we rationalize our pursuit of excessive desires, denying the presence of greed in our lives. As St. Francis de Sales notes, "No one will ever own themselves to be avaricious;—every one denies this contemptible vice:—men excuse themselves on the plea of providing for their children, or plead the duty of prudent forethought:—they never have too much, there is always some good reason for accumulating more; and even the most avaricious of men not only do not own to being such, but sincerely believe that they are not."

Generosity is an expression of mercy that involves giving to another person something of ours as an act of free will without obligation. We are invited to show generosity throughout our work with the Twelve Steps. Examples of generosity include service to others and a lack of attachment to our own time, material goods, or wants.

Envy vs. Admiration

Envy can be described as the active resentment of another's achievement or excellence to the extent that we wish to have it for ourselves. Envy stems from pride and can lead to separation from God, the Church, others, and our true sense of self. In the parable of the workers in the vineyard, Jesus poses the question, "Are you envious because I am generous?" (Mt 20:15).

Admiration entails gratitude for the gifts and blessings that God has given others. We can actively pursue the virtue of admiration by being of service to others. When we take this action and seek God in all things, we find God's glory reflected in our fellow brothers and sisters. St. Anselm of Canterbury summarizes the disposition we ought to take toward others: "If anyone else whom you love as much as yourself possessed the same blessedness, your joy would be doubled because you would rejoice as much for him as for yourself."

Wrath vs. Forgiveness

Wrath is a strong feeling of anger activated by a real or supposed injury. This feeling often shapes into an intense urge to act aggressively or take vengeance upon another. It is typically described as willing evil toward others and is a violent manifestation of harboring resentments. St. Paul implores that we "be angry but do not sin; do not let the sun set on your anger" (Eph 4:26).

In *The Book of Forgiving: The Fourfold Path for Healing Ourselves and Our World*, Archbishop Desmond Tutu and his daughter, Mpho Tutu, define *forgiveness* as "an intentional decision to release feelings of resentment or vengeance toward a person or group who has harmed you, regardless of whether they actually deserve it." It is important to add that forgiveness does not mean endorsing or approving wrongful behavior. In recovery, we receive forgiveness and mercy in fellowship with others, allowing us to extend the same mercy to ourselves and those around us. St. Augustine notes, "There are many kinds of alms, the giving of which helps us to obtain pardon for our sins; but none is greater than that by which we forgive from our heart a sin that someone has committed against us."

Lust vs. Chastity

Lust is the "disordered desire for or inordinate enjoyment of sexual pleasure" (*CCC* 2351). It includes a variety of attitudes and behaviors, such as viewing pornography, masturbating, overstepping another person's sexual boundaries, and entertaining fantasies or acting on desires to have sexual relations with someone who is not your spouse.

Chastity is the successful integration of sexuality within the person and thus the inner unity of our bodily and spiritual being. A healthy sexuality that is fostered through a reliance on prayer, the Twelve Steps, and sacramental grace yields balance, care, and love rather than coveting something precious that belongs to another. Chastity involves looking at others with dignity and a clean heart. We hear in the Beatitudes, "Blessed are the clean of heart, for they will see God" (Mt 5:8).

Gluttony vs. Asceticism

Gluttony is the excessive indulgence in food, drink, or other substances, or the demand for high-quality food and goods to an immoderate degree. We can be gluttonous about food, drink, video games, television, and many other indulgences that ultimately overwhelm our desire for God and become an idol.

Asceticism is the practice of denying physical or psychological gratification in order to attain a spiritual ideal or goal. When we fast or exercise temperance, we loosen our attachment to a substance or behavior. As St. Josemaría Escrivá conveys, "The body must be given a little less than it needs; otherwise, it will turn traitor."

Sloth/Acedia vs. Zeal

Sloth is a disinclination to action or labor; sluggishness; habitual indolence; laziness, idleness; slowness; delay. In spiritual terms, it is also known as *acedia* and can be defined as a "form of depression due to lax ascetical practice, decreasing vigilance, carelessness of heart" (*CCC* 2733). Worn down by the singular pursuit of our addictions and attachments, we lose the energy and desire to act for good. In terms of addiction, sloth is often characterized by feelings of hopelessness and doom. St. John Paul II provides insight into some mental distortions that give reasons for our inaction: "The fact is that attaining or realizing a higher value demands a greater effort of will. So in order to spare ourselves the effort, to excuse our failure to obtain this value, we minimize its significance." This happens slowly over time and can often go unnoticed while extreme depression is manifested.

Contrary to sloth, *zeal* is faith and love in action. A zealous heart finds excitement in pursuit of God's will and eagerly shares joy with others. As we have received blessings freely from others in recovery, we enthusiastically share a message of hope with those around us when an opportunity arises.

By completing our moral inventory, we acknowledge our need for God's mercy and forgiveness. Our inventory enables us to identify how to make things right as much as possible with those whom we've harmed, which we'll address in a later Step. And it's by exposing our faults and failings to the mercy of God—most powerfully in the Sacrament of Reconciliation—that we receive the grace to foster the virtues that help diminish our sinfulness and resist the cardinal vices. It's a process that never ends—but one that others in recovery, the Church, and Christ himself help us accomplish with faith, hope, and love.

Recovery Tool
There is a God—and it's not me.

Recovery Tool

Actions precede our change in attitude. If we pursue recovery with even half the zeal with which we have pursued our addictions, we will be in good shape.

Reflection Questions

Take time to think about and write down responses to the following questions. Once you've done so, discuss your responses with your sponsor and/or small workbook group.

- What sin have you habitually struggled with, and how has it affected your life?
- What virtue have you embraced? What growth did you experience as a result?

Prayer

The Memorare

Remember, O most gracious Virgin Mary,
that never was it known that anyone who fled to thy protection,
implored thy help, or sought thy intercession was left unaided.
Inspired by this confidence, I fly unto thee, O Virgin of virgins, my mother;
to thee do I come, before thee I stand, sinful and sorrowful.
O Mother of the Word Incarnate, despise not my petitions,
but in thy mercy hear and answer me.
Amen.

Putting the Steps into Action

This is where the real work of recovery takes place. Complete the following exercises before moving on to section 10:

☐ Sex and Finance Journal

☐ Seven Deadly Sins and Seven Recovering Virtues Exercise

 The work you're being asked to complete is not easy, and if you've made it this far, you've made it further than most who attempt recovery are willing to go. Keep moving forward one day, one section, and one step at a time! The following exercises are among the last that demand intensive writing.

Sex and Finance Journal

Getting to the root of our addictions, compulsions, and unhealthy attachments requires digging into all areas of our lives where our pursuits have gone astray or our responsibilities abandoned. Healthy integration of our sexual lives is an important part of the recovery process. We must also recognize where we've been unfaithful in our financial conduct. Allow the following questions to prompt personal reflection, and write out your responses in the space provided or on a separate sheet:

How has my pursuit of sexual relations damaged others, put others in harm's way, or destroyed my sense of self?

_____

_____

_____

_____

_____

Who would be hurt if they knew of any sexual behavior I do in secret?

_____

_____

_____

_____

_____

How have others and I been impacted by my unhealthy pursuit of sexual pleasure? How did I react when confronted?

_____

_____

_____

_____

_____

Have I demanded sexual arousal from others?

_____

_____

_____

_____

_____

Have I been honest with my spouse regarding my financial behavior?

_____

_____

_____

_____

_____

Have I stolen from others or been paid for work that I have not honestly completed?

_____

_____

_____

_____

Have I borrowed money recklessly without considering the impact of not paying the money back?

_____

_____

_____

_____

Do I live above my means, borrowing money or going into debt to support an unreasonable lifestyle?

_____

_____

_____

_____

Which of the seven deadly sins have contributed to my financial instability? Explain.

_____

_____

_____

_____

When have I been dishonest about my financial behavior?

_____

_____

_____

_____

Seven Deadly Sins and Seven Recovering Virtues Exercise

When completing a thorough moral inventory, we should strive for balance, acknowledging both assets and liabilities. Here we review our conduct through the lens of the seven capital vices and their corresponding recovering virtues. Reflect on the questions below and write about your findings.

Pride and Humility

Pride: An overly high opinion of oneself; exaggerated self-esteem; conceit, arrogance, vanity, self-satisfaction.
- Have I been so proud that I've been scorned (disrespected) as a braggart?
- Have I acted prideful, consciously or unconsciously, out of fear?
- Have I used pride to justify my excesses?
- Do I like to feel and act superior to others?

Humility: The acknowledgment that God is the author of all good. Humility avoids inordinate ambition or pride and provides the basis for turning to God in prayer.
- When do I put the needs of others ahead of my own desires and wishes for myself?
- How do I remain living in truth?
- Have I embraced and shared my frailties and mistakes while avoiding the role of victim?
- Do I actively give God and others credit for my success?

Greed and Generosity

Greed: An excessive desire for acquiring or having more than one needs or deserves.
- Have I been so greedy that I've been or could be labeled a thief?
- Do I long for the possessions of others out of fear of not getting enough?
- Do I let greed masquerade as ambition?

Generosity: An expression of mercy that involves giving to another person something of ours as an act of free will, without obligation.
- Do I treat others the way I would like to be treated?
- Have I sacrificed money, my reputation, and/or my desire for security and comfort for the sake of what is right and just?
- Do I share my time, personal space, money, talents, or other resources with others while expecting nothing in return?
- How am I of service to others?

Envy and Admiration

Envy: The active resentment of another's achievement, possessions, or excellence to the extent that we wish to have it for ourselves.
- Do I agonize over the chronic (persistent or recurring) pain of envy?
- Does seeing the ambitions of others materialize make me fear that mine haven't?

- Do I suffer from never being satisfied with what I have?
- Have I spent more time wishing for what others have than working toward those same achievements?

Admiration: This virtue entails gratitude for the gifts and blessings that God has given others.
- Do I genuinely show appreciation for things that are true, good, and beautiful?
- How do I express praise for God when impressed by nature's beauty, the goodwill of another, or good fortune that comes my way?
- Rather than falling into envy, have I been inspired to grow in virtue through my appreciation of another's gifts?

Wrath and Forgiveness

Wrath: A strong feeling of anger activated by a real or supposed injury, often shaped into an intense urge to act aggressively or take vengeance upon another; a violent manifestation of harboring resentment.
- Have I been angry enough to do physical injury to another person?
- Do I get angry out of fear when my instinctive demands are threatened?
- Have I enjoyed self-righteous anger in that many people annoy me and that makes me feel superior to them?
- Have I engaged in gossiping as a polite form of murder by character assassination?

Forgiveness: "An intentional decision to release feelings of resentment or vengeance toward a person or group who has harmed you, regardless of whether they actually deserve it" (Archbishop Tutu).
- For whom does my heart break?
- How do I share empathy with others?
- Is there a long-standing grudge that I have let go of or a broken relationship that no longer spurs feelings of resentment?
- When have I let go of an injustice as if it never even happened?

Lust and Chastity

Lust: A "disordered desire for or inordinate enjoyment of sexual pleasure" (CCC 2351).
- Have I been lustful to the point of overstepping another person's sexual boundaries?
- Do I fear I will never have the sex relations I feel I need?
- Do I have sex excursions that have been dressed up in dreams or delusions of romance?
- Do I covet another person's spouse or someone whom I am not in a romantic relationship with?

Chastity: The successful integration of sexuality within the person and thus the inner unity of our bodily and spiritual being.
- When have I experienced freedom to love myself and others without sexual attachment?
- How do I respect other people's sexual boundaries?
- What actions do I take to keep from viewing pornographic images and videos?

Gluttony and Asceticism

Gluttony: Excessive indulgence in food, drink, or other substances.
- Have I been gluttonous enough to harm my health?
- Do I grab for everything I can, fearing I'll never have enough?
- Do I bury myself in my work, hobbies, or other activities that I prefer, to the detriment of my responsibilities?

Asceticism: The practice of denying physical or psychological gratification in order to attain a spiritual ideal or goal.
- In what situations do I practice moderation in my behavior or thoughts?
- Do I voluntarily fast from items or behaviors that bring pleasure and comfort for the sake of a greater good?
- When have I renounced material possessions or detached myself from sensual pleasures?
- In what ways do I choose to delay gratification?

Sloth/Acedia and Zeal

Sloth: Disinclination to action or labor; sluggishness; habitual indolence; laziness, idleness; slowness; delay. In spiritual terms (*acedia*), it can be defined as a "form of depression due to lax ascetical practice, decreasing vigilance, carelessness of heart" (*CCC* 2733).
- Have I been paralyzed by sloth?
- Do I become alarmed or fearful at the prospect of work?
- Do I work hard with no better motive than to be secure and slothful later on?
- Do I loaf and procrastinate?
- Do I work grudgingly and under half steam?

Zeal: Faith and love in action; excitement in pursuit of God's will.
- What am I passionate about that brings joy to others and myself?
- What virtuous activities did I pursue before my addiction, compulsion, or unhealthy attachment settled in?
- What healthy routines and practices does my family engage in that I value?
- How do my actions speak of my love for God?

STEP 5

Admitted to God, to ourselves, and to another human being the exact nature of our wrongs.

ADMISSION TO GOD

The scorpion which has stung us is poisonous when it stings us, but when it is made into an oil it is an excellent remedy against its own sting; sin is shameful when we commit it, but when it is changed into confession and repentance, it is honorable and salutary. Contrition and confession are so beautiful and sweet-smelling, that they efface the ugliness and dissipate the stench of sin.

—St. Francis de Sales

Exploration and Understanding

Ann Marie's anorexia first reared its head when she was in high school, and during her senior year she lost so much weight that she ended up in an outpatient treatment center. She continued to struggle with anorexia after high school and well into adulthood. She learned to avoid social functions where she knew there would be food, tell people she had already eaten when she hadn't, and hide her feelings of depression, fear, and shame. It was also during these struggles that she grew distant from her Catholic upbringing and angry with God. "I knew all about surrendering from working the Steps, but it hadn't really set in because of the condition of my heart at that time. I was spiritually bankrupt," Ann Marie said.

After several years of appearing to manage on her own, the affliction emerged again. Ann Marie reconnected with her spiritual director and, along with her long time sponsor, started to work the Steps again in an intensive and spiritual manner. A grace-filled milestone occurred when, after many decades, she finally returned to Confession. "I went to the Sacrament of Reconciliation, which I had not done since seventh grade. I was working on Step 5 again. I had owned my mistakes and made all of my amends previously, but this time I did it with a priest, my spiritual director," Ann Marie said. "It was difficult and emotional, but he led me through it, and my spirituality, first slowly but then quickly, began to take off from there."

Admitting our sins to God is a crucial element of both recovery and our spiritual life in general. For it's by admitting our sins that we open ourselves up to receiving God's mercy and forgiveness. *Twelve Steps and Twelve Traditions* offers us a key insight about why Step 5 is so important in our recovery—those who remain free from addiction, compulsions, and unhealthy attachments are those who are willing to admit their faults to another. According to *Twelve Steps and Twelve Traditions*, humbly confessing our sins to another lets us experience four types of freedom and healing:

1. *Connection:* While we have experienced some level of connection since beginning our recovery and journeying with others, once we admit our faults to another—and find acceptance and solidarity—we encounter an even deeper sense of connection. We begin to feel a real sense of belonging, spurring kinship with others and God.

2. *Forgiveness:* We begin to realize that, no matter what we have done or thought, we can be forgiven. As we've faithfully worked on our moral inventory, we've come to see that "forgiveness was desirable, but it was only when we resolutely tackled Step Five that we inwardly knew we'd be able to receive forgiveness and give it, too" (pp. 57–58).

3. *Humility:* We begin moving toward humility by recognizing our defects and sins, thereby opening ourselves up to forgiveness from others and God. While it's true that we cannot correct or remove any defect unless we first see it, this isn't enough. It's only by sharing our faults and "being willing to take advice and accept direction [that we can] set foot on the road to straight thinking, solid honesty, and genuine humility" (p. 58).

4. *Direction:* Sharing with another person allows us to cut through our own rationalizations, wishful thinking, self-pity, and ego. Instead of being trapped in our deluded and solitary thoughts, we receive counsel, guidance, encouragement, and exhortation from another. This prevents us from continuing in our recovery and spiritual journey alone, which we must never do.

So, with whom should we choose to complete our Step 5? It's extremely important that we choose someone trustworthy, estimable, who has experience overcoming difficulties in their own lives, and with whom we can be open and honest. Often, this will be our sponsor, since this person should be ever-maturing in their own spiritual journey and understand the necessity of admitting our faults.

Yet, we may choose someone else, or perhaps do part of this Step with our sponsor and part of it with another person, such as a priest, counselor, or trusted friend. In fact, the person with whom we do Step 5 doesn't even have to be familiar with the Steps (though usually it helps if they are, or if they are well acquainted with the importance of confessing, as a priest would be). There might be a case where, for valid reasons, we don't feel we can reveal everything to our sponsor. Or we might simply want to do it with someone who has a similar history and/or temperament as us. This is fine. But remember, it's important to find someone, or a couple of people, to whom we can reveal *all of our* recorded defects.

We may find it quite difficult to be so honest with another human being, and this is understandable. Yet, there is a tremendous amount of peace, tranquility, and healing to be had when we open ourselves in this way. We'll likely find that once we start confessing to the other person, it gets easier and easier. "Many [in recovery], once agnostic or atheistic, tell us that it was during this stage of Step Five that they first actually felt the presence of

God. And even those who had faith already often become conscious of God as they never were before" (*Twelve Steps and Twelve Traditions*, p. 62).

As Catholics, we have the special gift of being able to share our wrongdoings not only with another person but also with a priest in the Sacrament of Reconciliation. This means that no matter who we choose to acknowledge our defects with to complete Step 5, we should also admit our sins to a priest in the Sacrament of Reconciliation if we haven't already done so.

The *Catechism of the Catholic Church* describes several components of the Sacrament of Reconciliation, which parallel our efforts in Steps 4 through 9:

- **Conversion**: We respond to Christ's call to reorient our lives and return to God.
- **Confession**: We disclose the nature of our wrongs to a priest, who fulfills the role of the Good Shepherd.
- **Forgiveness**: We receive forgiveness through the priest's absolution.
- **Penance**: We experience an interior transformation and a desire to move away from sin, which is expressed by external acts of reparation or satisfaction.
- **Reconciliation**: We establish right-relationship with God, others, and ourselves.

This is what Ann Marie experienced after she completed her Fifth Step and encountered God's mercy in the Sacrament of Reconciliation. She has been able to grow in holiness, allowing her past wounds and defects to be a means of grace to herself and others.

"My eating affliction is my wound, and it's the cross I'm called to embrace and the message I'm called to share with others," Ann Marie said. "I'm called to live with that wound but embrace the Lord. This wound is what brought me to my knees, to the Lord, and helped me learn to surrender to him. Today, I do his will and I have a beautiful, close, and loving relationship with God, for which I will be eternally grateful."

Let's consider the various steps of completing this powerful sacrament that has the power to take away all of our sins—including our most serious ones—and their connection with Steps 4 through 9.

Preparing for the Sacrament of Reconciliation

Before the sacrament:

- Preparing for Confession is a lot like conducting our searching and fearless moral inventory during the Fourth Step. Identifying where we have acted out of fear and resentment allows us to share the causes of our sinful behavior.
- Some have found it helpful to reference the Ten Commandments or the seven cardinal vices when examining their conscience prior to Reconciliation. Thorough preparation will enrich the experience and is an act of conversion in itself.

65

During the sacrament:

- Upon being greeted by the priest, we begin by saying: "Bless me, Father, for I have sinned. It has been [period of time] since my last Confession."
- We share with the priest behavior that has kept us distanced from God, confessing specific sins and how many times we recall committing them, as well as the motivation behind each sin. This is an act of the Fifth Step: "Admitting to God, ourselves, and another human being the exact nature of our wrongs." When we finish, the priest may offer spiritual direction or advice.

At the conclusion of the sacrament:

- The priest gives us an opportunity to offer an Act of Contrition (you can find the prayer below) or prayerful resolution to avoid sin. This overlaps with our Sixth Step willingness to allow God to remove all defects of character within us.
- It is helpful to find a quiet place to pray afterward and reflect on the forgiveness bestowed. You may wish to pray the Seventh Step Prayer (see page 102), humbly asking God to help you avoid sin in the future.

After the sacrament:

- We complete the penance given by the priest, which may include prayer and action. We pray for those whom we have wronged as well as those by whom we feel wronged.
- With a sponsor or spiritual director, we should determine if making amends is appropriate (Eighth Step). If so, we can make direct amends to such people, wherever possible, except when to do so would injure them or others (Ninth Step). However, we might not yet be in a position to make amends at this point in our recovery, and this should be something we discuss with our sponsor before taking action to make sure we're not jumping ahead too quickly.

It's worth acknowledging that we might have significant fears about returning to the Sacrament of Reconciliation or approaching it for the first time. Perhaps it's been several decades since we've received the sacrament, and we're anxious at the prospect of returning. We might wonder what the priest will think of us. Or we might worry that we'll be harshly judged. Or we might simply be confused about what to do and say.

It's normal to feel nervous about encountering a priest in this sacrament, but this shouldn't keep us from receiving the grace and forgiveness of God. The truth is that the priest has likely heard it all before! He is not there to judge us but to offer us the wonderful and compassionate mercy of Jesus. As so many come to find out, such an encounter with a priest can offer an incredible opportunity for tenderness and understanding.

As we've mentioned several times in this workbook already, it's by cooperating with God's grace—taking responsibility for our lives and having courage—that we come to know true freedom and healing. So, trust in the Lord and do not be afraid! He awaits all of us eagerly in the Sacrament of Reconciliation, delighting like the father of the prodigal son to pour his mercy upon us, no matter our sins or how far we've strayed from him.

Recovery Tool

We cannot give what we don't have. It's by receiving God's forgiveness that we become empowered to love and forgive ourselves and others.

Recovery Tool

Self-awareness without action can be dangerous. Knowledge of what's wrong without the capacity to change keeps us trapped in a helpless cycle. We need to act based on what we come to understand about our shortcomings or unhealthy tendencies.

Reflection Questions

Take time to think about and write down responses to the following questions. Once you've done so, discuss your responses with your sponsor and/or small workbook group.

- Describe your experience with Step 5. If you have not completed the Fifth Step, share about the fruits you have received from the Sacrament of Reconciliation.
- Make a commitment to the group to act upon Step 5:
  ◦ Whom will you ask for help?
  ◦ What questions or concerns do you have?
  ◦ If you are not prepared for this Step, update the group on what progress you are making.

Prayer
Act of Contrition

My God, I am sorry for my sins with all my heart.
In choosing to do wrong and failing to do good,
I have sinned against you whom I should love above all things.
I firmly intend, with your help, to do penance, to sin no more,
and to avoid whatever leads me to sin.
Our Savior Jesus Christ suffered and died for us.

In his name, my God, have mercy.
Amen.

Putting the Steps into Action

This is where the real work of recovery takes place. Complete the following before moving on to section 11:

☐ Schedule time with your sponsor or a trusted mentor and do your Fifth Step

 Prayerfully discern with whom you would like to complete your Fifth Step. Schedule at least an hour with that person, ensuring that the location provides comfort, privacy, and safety, and complete your Fifth Step before moving on to the next section. Additionally, participate in the Sacrament of Reconciliation with your Fourth and Fifth Steps as a guide.

STEP 6

*Were entirely ready to have
God remove all these defects
of character.*

SECTION 11

WILLINGNESS

The desire to improve, to strive always to surpass ourselves in order to grow in perfection is obviously indispensable. There is no question of abandoning it. To stop moving forward means to stop living. Anyone who doesn't want to become holy never will. Ultimately, God gives us what we desire, neither more nor less.

—Jacques Philippe, *Interior Freedom*

Exploration and Understanding

Being willing to allow God to remove our defects of character is not the same as expecting our reality and problems to disappear immediately. Remember, it's those types of expectations that got us into trouble in the first place with our addiction.

We hold in faith that God can and will heal us through his mercy, yet often the Lord chooses to do so gradually over time. A lucky few may have a "Damascus moment," during which they are immediately transformed. But the Lord usually invites us to cooperate with his grace steadily over time: "If we ask, God will certainly forgive our derelictions. But in no case does he render us white as snow and keep us that way without our cooperation. That is something we are supposed to be willing to work toward ourselves. He asks only that we try as best we know how to make progress in the building of character" (*Twelve Steps and Twelve Traditions*, p. 65). This idea is important because it's steeped in humility. It's an acceptance of our limitations and a willingness to allow God to change us how and when he desires. This is the posture of the saints. This is the posture of holiness.

In the book *Interior Freedom*, Fr. Jacques Philippe writes about our need to balance a striving toward holiness with accepting ourselves exactly as we are. "The desire to improve, to strive always to surpass ourselves in order to grow in perfection is obviously indispensable. . . . Anyone who doesn't want to become holy never will. Ultimately, God gives us what we desire, neither more nor less. But in order to become holy, we must accept ourselves as we are. These two statements are only apparently contradictory: both things are equally necessary, because they complement and balance each other" (p. 34).

We must do our part when it comes to recovery: complete the Step work, frequent the sacraments, spend time in prayer, make amends, serve others, and so on. Yet, as we affirm in the Sixth Step, we must at the same time embrace humility, acceptance, and openness. We must remember that only God has the power to remove our defects of character, forgive our sins, and heal us in our recovery.

After Elaine graduated from nursing school, she began taking NyQuil to help her sleep better. It worked. Realizing it would be easier to produce the same effect with alcohol, she began drinking wine on the rocks. So began her descent into alcoholism.

"I got my first nursing job, and the wine took me down in about a year. I remember walking out of the bar one day and realizing I didn't need anyone anymore since I had my bottle," Elaine said. After eventually landing in rehab, she experienced many years of sobriety. However, she relapsed when her dad suggested she might be able to drink beer casually. Then something happened.

"I got a beer Friday after work, but I told my daughter that I was going to church on Sunday. On that Friday I heard the Lord say that it was over and that he was coming for my beer. I knew it was jail, insanity, or death if I kept drinking. And so I drank that Friday and Saturday night and then blacked out and woke up to my little girl telling me that I had promised to take her to church on Sunday. And we went to church and the Holy Spirit touched me, and it was like being restored to sanity. I went home and the desire to drink was gone."

Elaine experienced an incredible gift in having her desire to drink removed. Yet, God was only able to do this after she did her part: after she was *willing* to seek him at church. She continued to seek him while accepting her need for him. She worked the Steps and found her way to the Catholic Church, where she eventually had an amazing healing experience in the Sacrament of Reconciliation. Elaine was willing to both seek the Lord and accept herself as she was. But to accept reality as it is and invite the Lord to heal us requires that we trust that the Lord actually wants to heal us. This is a form of "God-consciousness." Fr. Jacques Philippe illuminates this idea beautifully: "We urgently need the mediation of another's eyes to love ourselves and accept ourselves. The eyes may be those of a parent, a friend, a spiritual director; but above all they are those of God our Father. . . . The greatest gift given those who seek God's face by persevering in prayer may be that one day they will perceive something of this divine look upon themselves; they will feel themselves loved so tenderly that they will receive the grace of accepting themselves in depth" (p. 36).

We can only accept ourselves as we are by accepting that we are loved tenderly by God. When we do, we can experience the following:

- Acceptance of ourselves leads us to the acceptance of others.
- Through the Sacrament of Reconciliation, we encounter grace, love, acceptance, and forgiveness.

- Judgment fades when we practice accepting ourselves and others exactly as we are in this moment.
- Acceptance of our suffering opens us up to having God remove our defects of character.

When we accept our defects, sins, and suffering, God can transform us. We grow in holiness and love. But we place an obstacle in God's path when we are unwilling to accept our suffering, often because of fear. Fr. Jacques Philippe writes, "What really hurts is not so much suffering itself as the fear of suffering," and this fear "hardens us in self-protective, defensive attitudes, and often leads us to make irrational choices with disastrous consequences" (p. 47).

The good news is that when we're willing to seek holiness and accept ourselves exactly as we are—children loved by God—we begin to experience the Lord's healing and transformation in our lives.

Recovery Tool

We only increase our suffering by not accepting reality when it doesn't conform to our desires and will. Often, the fear of suffering is worse than suffering itself.

Recovery Tool

Criticism of our neighbor makes us perpetual victims, preventing God from healing and transforming us. While we need to take our own moral inventory, we don't need to take others'.

Reflection Questions

Take time to think about and write down responses to the following questions. Once you've done so, discuss your responses with your sponsor and/or small workbook group.

- What stands in the way of accepting yourself as you really are?
- How has being seen and loved by another in your life helped you understand how God sees you?
- Review the Simple Wisdom Worksheet on page 93. What recovery slogans and spiritual phrases help bring you peace, guidance, and acceptance?

Prayer

Prayer for Openness

God,

I stand before you with an open mind and an open heart.

I come ready to believe that you know what is best for me.

I am willing to shed all that you ask of me

so that my true self may be revealed to you and to others.

I continue to believe that your will for me is superior

to the plans that I have for myself.

I am ready to become new and clothed with the armor of your love.

Amen.

Putting the Steps into Action

This is where the real work of recovery takes place. Complete the following exercise before moving on to section 12:

☐ Simple Wisdom Worksheet

 Wisdom can be found all around us, especially as it has been revealed through the history of the Catholic Church throughout the ages. Now is a good time to explore various Catholic saints whom you might invite as an intercessor for your recovery journey as you continue through the Twelve Steps.

Simple Wisdom Worksheet

There are many slogans found in the rooms of 12-Step recovery, both hanging on the walls and coming from the mouths of wise old-timers. At first, these might seem trite and too simplistic to be applied to our complex lives and minds. However, you may discover that some of these sayings speak to you in a particular way on your recovery journey. If you've been around long enough, many of these are likely familiar to you. Add to the list others that come to your mind or are brought up by fellow group members.

- *Live and Let Live*
- *Let Go and Let God*
- *Easy Does It*
- *One Day at a Time*
- *Progress, Not Perfection*
- *First Things First*
- *Do the Next Right Thing*

For this exercise, write a description of what some of these common slogans mean to you. How is the slogan helpful, and how can you apply it to your life to make spiritual progress? Some of these sayings may overlap. Do not feel the need to describe each one, but more importantly, find a few slogans that resonate with you and might serve as a useful spiritual tool. There is room for you to add additional phrases.

Live and Let Live

My interpretation: _____

How I can apply to my life: _____

_____

_____

Let Go and Let God

My interpretation: _____

How I can apply to my life: _____

_____

_____

Easy Does It

My interpretation: _____

How I can apply to my life: _____

_____

One Day at a Time

My interpretation: _____

How I can apply to my life: _____

_____

_____

Progress, Not Perfection

My interpretation: _____

How I can apply to my life: _____

_____

_____

First Things First

My interpretation: _____

How I can apply to my life: _____

_____

_____

Do the Next Right Thing

My interpretation: _____

How I can apply to my life: _____

_____

_____

_____

My interpretation: _____

How I can apply to my life: _____

_____

_____

_____

My interpretation: _____

How I can apply to my life: _____

_____

_____

_____

My interpretation: _____

How I can apply to my life: _____

_____

_____

_____

My interpretation: _____

How I can apply to my life: _____

_____

_____

_____

My interpretation: _____

How I can apply to my life: _____

_____

_____

STEP 7

Humbly asked Him to remove our shortcomings.

SECTION 12
HUMILITY

If anyone would like to acquire humility, I can, I think, tell him the first step. The first step is to realize that one is proud. And a biggish step, too. At least, nothing whatever can be done before it. If you think you are not conceited, it means you are very conceited indeed.

—C. S. Lewis, *Mere Christianity*

Exploration and Understanding

In Step 7 we humbly accept our sinfulness and ask that God remove our shortcomings. By shortcomings we mean all our defects of character and propensities toward sin: our selfishness, sloth, narcissism, lust, callousness, greed, and more.

Humility is a necessary ingredient for this to happen. But humility doesn't mean groveling in the dirt, allowing ourselves to be walked all over or treated poorly. It certainly doesn't involve self-hatred or self-disgust. Sometimes people assume this is what it means to be humble. These are examples of false humility since they deny the inherent dignity we've been given as children of God. In other words, this type of thinking elevates our own judgment above God's, resulting in yet another manifestation of our ego!

True humility is accepting *who we are as we are*: a beloved, dignified child of God who is also sinful, broken, and in need of grace. What does this look like in practice?

- Taking responsibility for the harm we've caused others.
- Seeing ourselves as well as others as worthy of respect and love.
- Accepting that we don't have everything figured out—and that we don't need to.
- Standing regularly before God and admitting our sinfulness and need for his mercy.

Jesus gives us a powerful example of humility when he tells of the tax collector standing "at a distance [who] would not even raise his eyes to heaven but beat his breast and prayed, 'O God, be merciful to me a sinner'" (Lk 18:13). According to Jesus, it was this man—not the self-righteous Pharisee who thanked God for not being sinful like the rest of humanity—who went home justified by his prayer.

A wonderful recovery resource is the book *Drop the Rock: Removing Character Defects*, by Bill P., Todd W., and Sara S. The authors emphasize an important element of humility, which is becoming and remaining *teachable*.

"Open-mindedness is a very important part of humility. We don't know it all. There is still more we can learn. And maybe even more importantly, some need to unlearn. Yet, how many of us in the Program aren't open to new ideas and thoughts? Especially after having been around awhile, how many do we see who continue to say and do the exact same things year after year? It seems that many of us resist a clear idea of humility so we don't have to conform to it" (p. 59).

While sitting around a campfire as a teenager, Jon realized what alcohol could do for him. After a few beers, he could become someone else—someone funny, good with girls, charming, and self-confident—the type of person he had always wanted to be.

"I was one of those people who could be blackout drunk and have a conversation with you and you would have no idea. I drank during the first eight years of my marriage, and my wife had no idea that I was blackout drunk most of the time," Jon said. He eventually began drinking every morning. It got so bad that for an entire month he failed to report to work.

"I worked in the architectural design community, and my drinking really affected my life at this point," Jon said. "They would have fired me if I had shown up to work to allow them to fire me, but I drank in my basement the entire last month of that year. It was then that I realized I needed help and entered a drug and alcohol rehab facility, where I spent five days detoxing."

It was in rehab that God acted. "I got on my knees at that facility and asked God to please help me, and I heard him say to me, 'All you had to do was ask.' These are the words I actually heard on that day in that room. And from then on my drive to drink was lifted from me. I believe that God had a direct hand in my recovery," Jon shared.

God responded to Jon because he accepted his need for grace—he admitted with humility that he couldn't help himself.

As we discussed in the previous section, God can and does heal people of certain defects immediately. But even if he does, there will always be other defects of character that we'll need to work on over time. We'll need to continue to work the Steps, trusting God's mercy throughout our recovery. We read the following in *Drop the Rock*: "In recovery, we try to take the opposite of our character defects and shortcomings and turn them into principles. For example, we work to change fear into faith, hate into love, egoism into humility, anxiety and worry into serenity, complacency into action, denial into acceptance, jealousy into trust, fantasy into reality, selfishness into tolerance, despair into hope, self-hate into self-respect, and loneliness into fellowship" (xvii).

This aligns with our spiritual conversion as well. In the *Catechism of the Catholic Church*, we read that "conversion is accomplished in daily life by gestures of reconciliation, concern for the poor, the exercise and defense of justice and right, by the admission of faults to one's brethren, fraternal correction, revision of life, examination of conscience, spiritual direction, acceptance of suffering, endurance of persecution for the sake of righteousness" (1435). In other words, when we ask God to remove our defects of character, we must approach him with an authentic desire to change our lives, trust that God can indeed help us, commit to working the Steps, and seek continual conversion in the Church.

This is what Jon did. After detoxing, Jon began attending 12-Step meetings regularly. The group he attended met seven days a week at 6:15 a.m. in the morning. He didn't miss a single session for an entire year and a half. His commitment paid off, and he hasn't had a drink since he entered that detox facility almost twenty years ago. Eventually, Jon and his wife helped start a Catholic in Recovery group in Columbus, Ohio, supporting others on their journey of recovery and conversion with the necessary spirit of humility.

To conclude, let's consider our great model of humility in the Church, the Blessed Mother. When she was approached by the angel, she humbly submitted to the Lord's will. Her great fiat—that wonderful yes—allowed Christ to be born into a world in need of his mercy and salvation. We can learn to become humble like our mother by reciting and meditating on her wonderful hymn of praise for the Lord, known as the Magnificat:

> My soul proclaims the greatness of the Lord;
>   my spirit rejoices in God my savior.
> For he has looked upon his handmaid's lowliness;
>   behold, from now on will all ages call me blessed.
> The Mighty One has done great things for me,
>   and holy is his name.
> His mercy is from age to age
>   to those who fear him.
> He has shown might with his arm,
>   dispersed the arrogant of mind and heart.
> He has thrown down the rulers from their thrones
>   but lifted up the lowly.
> The hungry he has filled with good things;
>   the rich he has sent away empty.
> He has helped Israel his servant,
>   remembering his mercy,
> according to his promise to our fathers,
>   to Abraham and to his descendants forever. (Lk 1:46–55)

Holy Mary, Mother of God, pray for us that we may approach Step 7 with your same spirit of humility and trust!

Recovery Tool
Humility is knowing *who* and *whose* we are.

Recovery Tool

Our healing is not just for the sake of ourselves, but also for the purpose of serving God and others.

Reflection Questions

Take time to think about and write down responses to the following questions. Once you've done so, discuss your responses with your sponsor and/or small workbook group.

- Who is a model of humility for you? Describe how their actions help you form patterns of humility and increase self-acceptance.
- How do you maintain daily conversion?
- Which of your character defects can you change into spiritual principles?

Prayer

Seventh Step Prayer from *Alcoholics Anonymous*

My Creator,
I am now willing that you should have all of me,
the good and bad.
I pray that you now remove from me
every single defect of character
which stands in the way of my usefulness
to you and my fellows.
Grant me strength, as I go out from here,
to do your bidding.
Amen.

Putting the Steps into Action

This is where the real work of recovery takes place. Complete the following before moving on to section 13:

☐ Daily Conversion Reflection

☐ Meditate on the Magnificat, and ask the Blessed Mother for the grace to approach Step 7 with humility

☐ Pray the Seventh Step Prayer each day for at least a week or until you commit it to memory

Visit the digital platform at www.catholicinrecovery.com/cirworkbook to watch videos of others sharing how they have approached the Blessed Virgin Mary and found her aid in overcoming addictions, compulsions, and unhealthy attachments.

Daily Conversion Reflection

> Conversion is accomplished in daily life by gestures of reconciliation, concern for the poor, the exercise and defense of justice and right, by the admission of faults to one's brethren, fraternal correction, revision of life, examination of conscience, spiritual direction, acceptance of suffering, endurance of persecution for the sake of righteousness.
>
> —*Catechism of the Catholic Church*, 1435

Spend time reflecting on each of these actions of daily conversion, putting your understanding of each in your own words and getting specific about how each would take shape in your life.

Gestures of reconciliation: _____

_____

_____

Concern for the poor: _____

_____

_____

Exercise and defense of justice and right: _____

_____

_____

Admission of faults to one's brethren: _____

_____

_____

Fraternal correction: _____

_____

_____

Revision of life: _____

_____

_____

STEP 8

Made a list of all persons we
had harmed,
and became willing to make
amends to them

Examination of conscience: _____

_____

_____

Spiritual direction: _____

_____

_____

Acceptance of suffering: _____

_____

_____

Endurance of persecution for the sake of righteousness:

_____

_____

_____

STEP 8

*Made a list of all persons we
had harmed,
and became willing to make
amends to them all.*

SECTION 13

CHRISTIAN LOVE

If possible, on your part, live at peace with all.

—Romans 12:18

Exploration and Understanding

We're now ready to begin the process of making amends to those we've harmed. However, in Step 8 we are not actually making amends yet—that will be the next Step. Rather, we are prayerfully constructing an "amends list" of people we've harmed. In this Step, we are taking concrete actions to begin restoring harmony with those we've harmed by our addictive behaviors, lies, and selfishness.

This Step can be difficult for a couple of reasons. First, it requires that we demonstrate humility and self-awareness to admit to ourselves how we've failed to love another person. It's often easier to rationalize, downplay, and excuse our harmful actions.

Second, there will inevitably be people we have harmed who have also harmed us. As a result, we may harbor deep-seated resentments toward them, which can block us from interior healing and an authentic willingness to make amends. But remember, we're making a list of those we've harmed in this Step—not a list of those who have harmed us!

Because there can be serious difficulties and pitfalls during this Step, it's critical to work closely with our sponsors. Our sponsors can prevent us from falling into self-pity, resentment, and feelings of self-righteousness. Our sponsors can ensure we're not rationalizing or excusing the harm we've caused others. And our sponsors can make sure we're not rushing through this Step, and that we don't progress to making amends before we're ready (which can be a *major* temptation).

The good news is that we've already done much of the work for this Step: we did it when we completed our moral inventories during Step 4. In this Step, we're simply identifying the people from those inventories and determining our readiness to make amends to them.

> Let's look at Steps 8 and 9. We have a list of all persons we have harmed and to whom we are willing to make amends. We made it when we took inventory. We subjected ourselves to a drastic self-appraisal. Now we go out to our fellows and repair the damage done in the past. We attempt to sweep away the debris which has accumulated

out of our effort to live on self-will and run the show ourselves. If we haven't the will to do this, we ask until it comes. (*Alcoholics Anonymous*, p. 76)

While a sponsor can help ensure we're not blaming others or projecting our own resentments on others unfairly, it's worth stating again that we may indeed have people on our lists who have objectively and legitimately harmed us in serious ways. And it's understandable that we may have no desire to make amends with some of these people.

In *Alcoholics Anonymous*, better known as the Big Book, we read about approaching a person who "has done us more harm than we have done him" (p. 77). But what solution is given? After much humble prayer, we are to "take the bit in our teeth" and go to the person in a "helpful and forgiving spirit, confessing our former ill feeling and expressing our regret" (p. 77). In other words, we humbly admit the wrongs we have committed, seeking the other's forgiveness, and do our best to model our Lord on the Cross, the ultimate example of Christian love. St. Aelred of Rievaulx gives us a beautiful meditation on Christ's willingness to forgive even those who crucified him.

> Father, forgive them, for they do not know what they are doing. They are great sinners, yes, but they have little judgment; therefore, Father, forgive them. They are nailing me to the cross, but they do not know who it is that they are nailing to the cross: if they had known, they would never have crucified the Lord of glory; therefore, Father, forgive them. They think it is a lawbreaker, an impostor claiming to be god, a seducer of the people. I have hidden my face from them, and they do not recognize my glory; therefore, Father, forgive them, for they do not know what they are doing.

To foster this Christian love toward others, especially those who have seriously harmed us, we'll need to pray regularly for them. Even if we don't feel a desire to pray for them, that's okay. We can pray for the desire to pray for them. We can pray for the willingness to make amends to them even if we don't yet have it. We can pray for the grace to love unconditionally with the same love Christ has for us even though we are lacking it.

Even after much prayer, there may be certain people on our amends list to whom we aren't yet ready to make amends. We might still harbor too much ill feeling and require more time for prayer. Or there may be certain people that we cannot or should not approach since it would cause more harm than good to that person and/or ourselves. It's only through regular prayer and close collaboration with our sponsor that we can determine this.

Organizing an Eighth Step Amends List

Note: There are many ways to approach making an amends list for Step 8. Here we provide instructions for one way of completing it; or you can use the templated worksheet on page 112. However, if your sponsor prefers another way for working this Step, feel free to use their approach instead.

Make three columns with the following headers: *Easy*, *Moderate*, and *Hard*. In the *Easy* column we'll list the names of people we're willing to make amends to right now. These are people with whom we feel interiorly able and willing to make amends today if we had to. In the *Moderate* column we'll list people for whom we will require more time, and more interior conversion, before being willing to make amends. In the *Hard* column we'll list the people to whom we cannot imagine ever being willing to make amends. These are the people we'll need to pray for more intentionally, asking God for the grace to soften our hearts toward them.

Now we'll refer back to our Resentment Inventory and Sex and Finance Journal to identify which individuals—close family, friends, coworkers, etc.—we've harmed and list them in one of the three columns. We'll add as many rows as we have names. Below are questions to consider as we're determining whom to add to our list:

- With whom did we break trust?
- Whom did our lies, deceit, and dishonesty affect?
- Who was the object of our anger, insecurity, shame, and fear?
- What financial amends are owed?
- How did our sexual conduct harm another?

Once we've finished our amends list, we'll commit to praying every day for each person listed for *at least* two to three weeks. We might not mean it or feel anything when we pray for certain people, but we'll pray for them anyway, trusting that the Lord can and will soften our hearts and help us become willing to make amends to them in the next Step.

Finally, let's consider what to do when a person on our list is deceased or unreachable. While we won't be able to make a traditional amends to such a person, there are still things we can do to make a spiritual or ritualistic amends. For example, we can request that the person be remembered at a particular Mass and make plans to attend that Mass and pray for them. We can also prayerfully write a letter to the person, detailing what we would say if we could make amends in their presence. Depending on the situation, we might choose to save the letter, destroy it, or even recite its contents at their gravesite. Take some time to consider how you can make a spiritual amends with those on your list whom you cannot see again in person.

By the grace of God and our commitment to working this Step faithfully with our sponsors, we can truly acquire the willingness to make amends without expecting anything in return—to admit our faults without pointing out another's wrongs or offenses. In the spirit of Christian love, we can "sweep our side of the street" without demanding or manipulating others to sweep their side, too.

> ### *Recovery Tool*
> **Making amends is the greatest action we can take—to get right with our neighbor with no expectation of receiving anything in return.**

> ### *Recovery Tool*
> **We must guard against resenting ourselves because we are unwilling to forgive ourselves.**

Reflection Questions

Take time to think about and write down responses to the following questions. Once you've done so, discuss your responses with your sponsor and/or small workbook group.

- How have you experienced reconciliation with others?
- How do you feel about making amends with others, even those who are also at fault?
- What experience do you have praying for those you dislike or who dislike you?

Prayer

Prayer from Thomas Merton

My Lord God,
I have no idea where I am going. I do not see the road ahead of me.
I cannot know for certain where it will end.
Nor do I really know myself,
and the fact that I think I am following your will
does not mean that I am actually doing so.
But I believe that the desire to please you does in fact please you.
And I hope I have that desire in all that I am doing.
I hope that I will never do anything apart from that desire.
And I know that if I do this you will lead me by the right road,
though I may know nothing about it.
Therefore will I trust you always
though I may seem to be lost and in the shadow of death.
I will not fear, for you are ever with me,
and you will never leave me to face my perils alone.
Amen.

Putting the Steps into Action

This is where the real work of recovery takes place. Complete the following exercise before moving on to section 14:

☐ Eighth Step Amends Worksheet

 Begin praying for those on your amends list every day for the next three weeks, preparing your heart to make amends. You may choose to focus your prayer on those for whom you have the most lingering resentment or the people with whom you are especially unwilling to make amends.

Eighth Step Amends Worksheet

1. As we prepare to make direct amends with those whom we have harmed, we must first make a clear list of where amendment is needed. The best place to begin is your Fourth Step Resentment Inventory. Add others where amendment is needed, considering your Sex and Finance Journal and the Eighth Step Amends List provided earlier in this section. Organize your list based on how challenging you think it will be to make an honest amends without discussing the other's faults, adding them under *Easy*, *Moderate*, or *Hard* below.
2. Begin praying for those on your amends list, focusing on those whom you are especially challenged to make an amends to. Ask God to be present to them and that they may know their identity as his beloved son or daughter.
3. Share your list with a sponsor or companion in recovery to discern what amends are necessary, discuss where you've gone wrong, and decide in what cases making amends would injure the subject or others.
4. Continue to add names as they come to mind, and ask God to grant you clarity, courage, and guidance along the way.

Easy	Moderate	Hard

STEP 9

Made direct amends to such people wherever possible, except when to do so would injure them or others.

STEP 9

Made direct amends to such people wherever possible, except when to do so would injure them or others.

SECTION 14
FORGIVENESS

Then Peter approaching asked him, "Lord, if my brother sins against me, how often must I forgive him? As many as seven times?" Jesus answered, "I say to you, not seven times but seventy-seven times."

—Matthew 18:21–22

Exploration and Understanding

Now that we have completed our amends list, we're ready to work closely with our sponsor on approaching the people with whom we're ready to make amends—to restore harmony to those whose peace of mind we have stolen. Remember, though, that just because we've completed our list does not mean we're ready to make amends to everyone on it. Not only might we need more time for prayer and internal healing before we can do so, but we'll also need to practice making amends with our sponsor.

Throughout all of this, we should continue to pray for those on our list, asking for the grace to forgive those who have harmed us as well. Rev. Martin Luther King Jr. taught that those who are devoid of the power to forgive are devoid of the power to love. The goal is to tenderize our hearts, and this can only occur through the grace of forgiveness received and given.

In the previous section we touched on the importance of forgiving those on our amends list who have also harmed us. We must pray fervently for this grace; we won't know true healing unless we are able to forgive others as God forgives us. As Jesus instructs us, we are to forgive others not merely "seven times but seventy-seven times" (Mt 18:22). In other words, we are called to forgive without measure or limit. Let's not forget that when Jesus modeled for us how to pray to the Father, he made sure to include forgiveness: "forgive us our sins for we ourselves forgive everyone in debt to us" (Lk 11:4). St. John Paul II reminded us in his message for the 1997 World Day of Peace, "Forgiveness can seem contrary to human logic, which often yields to the dynamics of conflict and revenge. But forgiveness is inspired by the logic of love—that love which God has for every man and woman."

Forgiving others is challenging for a variety of reasons, including these:

- It requires us to act contrary to the way we might feel.
- It requires that we let go of injuries freely without any expectation of reward.
- It's an ongoing process that requires continual prayer, action, and humility.

God's command to forgive doesn't only extend to those who've harmed us on our amends list—it extends to ourselves as well. We are called to love others as we love ourselves, and this means forgiving ourselves for the harm we've caused. If God has forgiven us—and he has if we've asked for it as we've worked the Steps and participated in the Sacrament of Reconciliation—then we must forgive ourselves.

Self-forgiveness is an inside job. While prayer is always the surest way to foster it, here are some other approaches to help us acknowledge our need to forgive ourselves and do so:

- Meditate on how deeply hurt we have been by our own troubling behavior and our need to be forgiven for it.
- Consider the actions we are taking to make a real change in our lives and that God is directing these changes.
- Recall our identity as a beloved child of God.
- Recognize and reflect on the unhealthy and harsh thoughts we might have about ourselves. Would you speak to another person this way? How can you respond to yourself with love and compassion instead of with harmful self-talk?
- Spend time with people who pour love and forgiveness into you to be reminded of your inherent dignity.

Practicing Step 9 with Your Sponsor

Ann started drinking when she was fourteen. "My family had a history of addiction. I remember the first time I took a drink it seemed like I had finally found a solution to my problems," she shared. As a child, Ann was very close to her siblings and parents, especially since they moved a lot. But when two of her older siblings became ensnared by addiction, her family was destabilized, causing her much pain and confusion.

"I reacted to this pain by trying to make things okay for people in my family. If I could just make everyone I loved okay, then I thought I would be okay, which was codependent behavior. But when I took that first drink as a teenager, I felt like the world was fine. It stopped the voice telling me I had to make everyone else okay. I liked that feeling, so I followed it for years," Ann said.

This continued until her late forties, when her drinking intensified. "I was trying to manage being a good stay-at-home mom and wife so that I would have value in the world, but it was mostly about looking good on the outside while on the inside I was dying. I was a hidden drinker. Every day I would get up, aware that my drinking was harming my relationship with my family and God, and tell myself I needed a little bit of alcohol and that I would stop tomorrow. I was trapped, and that was my bottom."

Ann tried to find healing on her own by reading books on recovery and relying on self-will. It didn't work. It wasn't until she finally entered a recovery program and found a sponsor—a woman who exuded serenity and joy—that she started to experience true healing.

"My sponsor knew how to work with a codependent alcoholic like me," Ann said.

Once we're ready to make amends to someone on our list, it's now time to practice. We strongly encourage you to work closely with your sponsor, role-playing making your amends so that they can offer advice, feedback, and encouragement. You'll need to plan exactly what you're going to say and how you want to say it well before you actually make your amends with the person.

It can also be helpful to write a "do not send" letter. This is a letter in which we write everything we'd like to share with the person on our amends list—a letter that we won't actually send to the person—that can help clarify our thoughts and feelings. It helps us focus on what we should and shouldn't say while making our amends. We then show this letter to our sponsor and review it with them.

It's essential to practice with our sponsor because there are many potential pitfalls to this Step. Making amends is not telling the person we forgive them (this might only further offend them!) or asking them to forgive us. It isn't about making ourselves feel better, either, or excusing ourselves from past hurts simply because we've admitted them. These are both examples of the type of unhealthy thinking that often fueled our addiction—examples of victim or controlling mentalities. And these are precisely the things a sponsor can point out to us through practice.

Here is what we should be doing when we make amends:

- Point out and admit to the wrongs we have committed.
- Share what we are doing to correct these wrongs (our tangible solutions to them—our commitment to a 12-Step program, our involvement in our parish, etc.).
- Ask the person if they have any feedback for us to help us grow.

This may look simple. But don't overlook the temptation to defend ourselves if we're attacked, point out the other's wrongs, or downplay our role in the harm done. By anticipating these possibilities and practicing with our sponsor, we limit the chances of them occurring and derailing our amends. We'll have prepared ourselves to approach the person with no expectation of receiving anything in return, be that an apology, forgiveness, or even the healing of the relationship. If harmony is restored, praise be to God! If not, that's okay—we are only asked to sweep our side of the street. And if we have prayed and practiced faithfully during Step 8 and Step 9, we can safely leave the outcome to God.

Through working the Steps with her sponsor and deepening her commitment to prayer and the sacraments, Ann embarked on the path toward healing. When it came to making her amends, she realized recovery was more than simply saying sorry.

"The greatest amends I could offer to those I had harmed was to immerse myself in a recovery program and get sober so that I could change the dynamics of my family. One of the things I did as a mother when I was drinking was that I forced my children to be 'okay' so that I could be 'okay,' even though I wasn't. I've realized that making a living amends means letting my children live their own lives and not trying to control them to make myself feel better. It means loving them and having compassion on them while handing them over to God. God changes us so much when we live out our amends—the healing that happened in my life and family has been an amazing grace," Ann said.

Recovery Tool

It isn't our words but our actions that matter. Often our words have been dishonest or have been tools of control, manipulation, and selfishness.

Recovery Tool

We don't think our way into right behavior. We act our way into right thinking.

Reflection Questions

Take time to think about and write down responses to the following questions. Once you've done so, discuss your responses with your sponsor and/or small workbook group.

- How have you experienced forgiveness from God and others?
- What challenges hinder your efforts to forgive yourself?
- How have you sought "revenge" on yourself in the past?
- What actions can you take to begin planting the seeds of forgiveness for yourself and others?

The Lord's Prayer

Our Father, who art in heaven,
hallowed be thy name.
Thy kingdom come.
Thy will be done on earth, as it is in heaven.
Give us this day our daily bread,
and forgive us our trespasses,

as we forgive those who trespass against us,
and lead us not into temptation,
but deliver us from evil.
Amen.

Putting the Steps into Action

This is where the real work of recovery takes place. Complete the following before moving on to section 15:

☐ Review Eighth Step Amends Worksheet with your sponsor and / or small workbook group

☐ Continue praying for those on your amends list

 As you are planning to make amends, consider things such as how you will prepare and with whom you will begin. Perhaps you will first write a "do not send" letter. Make plans to practice role-playing making amends with another person before going live.

as we forgive those who trespass against us,
and lead us not into temptation,
but deliver us from evil.
Amen.

...ing The Steps Into Action

...Rules / Friends Worksheet with your sponsor and/or small workbook group

SECTION 15

JUSTICE

The just man, often mentioned in the Sacred Scriptures, is distinguished by habitual right thinking and the uprightness of his conduct toward his neighbor.

—*Catechism of the Catholic Church* 1807

Exploration and Understanding

We're now ready to meet with the people on our amends list individually (in person if possible, though over the phone or online if not) and—with a spirit of humility and justice—admit our wrongdoings to them. Again, before continuing with this Step, ensure you have consistently prayed for them, have practiced making amends with your sponsor, and have your sponsor's blessing to proceed. If you don't feel ready yet (or your sponsor doesn't think you are), that's okay. Continue praying for the people on your list and working with your sponsor. Likely, there will be some people you are ready to meet with now and others for whom you need more preparation. While we don't want to delay or procrastinate in completing this Step, it's important to realize that it may take time to make amends with everyone on our list, especially those in the "Hard" column.

To complete this Step is to act justly. We are making right what we have wronged and owe our neighbor to the extent possible. We are attempting to restore trust that we have sundered. We are restoring peace where we have sown strife. In some cases, it may be necessary and appropriate to provide material or financial restoration to the person (this is something to be prayed about and discussed with your sponsor).

Much of the work we've been doing throughout this workbook has been to form within us the "habitual right thinking" mentioned in the quote above from the *Catechism of the Catholic Church* (1807). In fact, while justice is certainly a major aspect of Step 9, working the Twelve Steps helps strengthen within us what the Church teaches are the four cardinal virtues. We grow in holiness when we combine the four cardinal virtues with the three theological virtues—faith, hope, and love—that we receive in Baptism as we become members of Christ's Body.

The Four Cardinal Virtues

> *Prudence* is the virtue that disposes practical reason to discern our true good in every circumstance and to choose the right means of achieving it; "the prudent man looks where he is going." . . . Prudence is "right reason in action," writes St. Thomas Aquinas, following Aristotle. . . .
>
> *Justice* is the moral virtue that consists in the constant and firm will to give [one's] due to God and neighbor. Justice toward God is called the "virtue of religion." Justice toward men disposes one to respect the rights of each and to establish in human relationships the harmony that promotes equity with regard to persons and to the common good. . . .
>
> *Fortitude* is the moral virtue that ensures firmness in difficulties and constancy in the pursuit of the good. It strengthens the resolve to resist temptations and to overcome obstacles in the moral life. The virtue of fortitude enables one to conquer fear, even fear of death, and to face trials and persecutions. It disposes one even to renounce and sacrifice his life in defense of a just cause. . . . .
>
> *Temperance* is the moral virtue that moderates the attraction of pleasures and provides balance in the use of created goods. It ensures the will's mastery over instincts and keeps desires within the limits of what is honorable. . . . In the New Testament it is called "moderation" or "sobriety." We ought "to live sober, upright, and godly lives in this world." (CCC 1806–1809)

As for making amends and completing Step 9, here are some things to keep in mind:

- While we should never be afraid to mention our faith in Christ, it's important that we don't wield it as a weapon when making our amends. *Alcoholics Anonymous* reminds us that it's "seldom wise to approach an individual, who still smarts from our injustice to him, and announce that we have gone religious" (p. 76). The goal is to make things right, not to convince others that we've undergone transformational spiritual discoveries and deserve forgiveness or acceptance because we're new people now (p. 77).

- This doesn't mean we hide our faith. As Peter tells us, we should "always be ready to give an explanation to anyone who asks you for a reason for your hope, but do it with gentleness and reverence" (1 Pt 3:15). We should invite the Holy Spirit to guide our speech before meeting with the person.

- It bears repeating that under no circumstances are we to point out the other's wrongs, demand an apology, or expect forgiveness or approval from them. We do not expect to receive anything other than the grace of knowing we've done our part.

- We may hope for but not expect to be blessed with an encounter of healing. The other person may offer us forgiveness or even admit to their wrongs against us. We can pray for such restoration and harmony, but, again, we must never expect a specific outcome.

Alcoholics Anonymous offers us encouragement on this last point: "Sometimes the man we are calling upon admits his own fault, so feuds of years' standing melt away in an hour.

Rarely do we fail to make satisfactory progress. Our former enemies sometimes praise what we are doing and wish us well. Occasionally, they will offer assistance. It should not matter, however, if someone does throw us out of his office. We have made our demonstration, done our part. It's water over the dam" (p. 78).

Even if our act of making amends doesn't go well at all and the person throws us out of the office, if we have done our part with humility, then we can rest assured that we've made good on our responsibility to make amends with that person.

We should also acknowledge that there may be certain wrongs we've committed that we cannot make right. We are not going to be able to fix every past mistake or restore every broken relationship. But this is never our goal anyway, since we've come to realize that it's God alone who brings healing and harmony—not our own efforts. Yes, we must do our part in making amends. But we do so with the humble acknowledgment that it's ultimately God who redeems and makes all things new.

María started having wine and beer at family gatherings and dinner parties in her late twenties for one reason: she wanted to feel like she belonged. Within six months, her drinking had become a problem, controlling her thinking and actions. "I began drinking in secret," María shared, "which only produced more shame and guilt. I began hating the person I had become."

María eventually participated in a retreat where she was struck profoundly by a talk from a nun who was also a recovering alcoholic. "The Lord knew that I needed to know I wasn't alone in my drinking and that there was hope for recovery and healing."

In time María surrendered to God and became honest with herself about her drinking. With the help of the Twelve Steps, the Eucharist, the Sacrament of Reconciliation, scripture, the Rosary, and the saints, she slowly began to receive healing on the road of recovery.

María experienced particularly crucial interior healing when she worked Step 9.

She prepared to make amends by creating index cards with a person's name on one side and the way or ways she had wronged them on the other side. She then went through each one with her sponsor, practicing making amends. Although she was worried she wouldn't always know what to say or that the person might become angry or reject her, her sponsor reminded her that all of that was out of her control. She only needed to sweep her side of the street, leaving everything else in God's hands. Still, María was nervous, especially about making amends to a life long friend. "I was terrified about how things would unfold. I was preparing myself to be rejected."

When María finally made her amends to this particular friend, the woman broke down in tears and thanked María for the gift of their friendship, which had brought much joy to her life. "Making a thorough amends to her helped her to see my sincerity and how much I valued her as well," María said.

It was still a difficult process, yet one that proved fruitful. "Thankfully, in every case of making amends, I felt like more of a woman taking responsibility for my life and for my mistakes. It is difficult to make amends to another person, but it is one of the most empowering things I have ever done for myself," she said.

To end this section, let's turn to the Big Book's Ninth Step Promises, which is a wonderful and encouraging reminder that if we proceed through this Step virtuously and with God's grace, we will come to know deep-seated freedom, healing, and joy.

> If we are painstaking about this phase of our development, we will be amazed before we are half way through. We are going to know a new freedom and a new happiness. We will not regret the past nor wish to shut the door on it. We will comprehend the word serenity and we will know peace. No matter how far down the scale we have gone, we will see how our experience can benefit others. That feeling of uselessness and self-pity will disappear. We will lose interest in selfish things and gain interest in our fellows. Self-seeking will slip away. Our whole attitude and outlook upon life will change. Fear of people and of economic insecurity will leave us. We will intuitively know how to handle situations which used to baffle us. We will suddenly realize that God is doing for us what we could not do for ourselves. (*Alcoholics Anonymous*, pp. 83–84)

Recovery Tool

We don't worry about wrongs that cannot be made right as long as we have a desire to make them right if we could.

Reflection Questions

Take time to think about and write down responses to the following questions. Once you've done so, discuss your responses with your sponsor and/or small workbook group.

- Describe how the Twelve Steps and the sacraments have helped you make spiritual progress in one of the cardinal virtues: prudence, justice, fortitude, and temperance.
- Which of the four cardinal virtues do you desire to develop more intentionally? How might you do so?
- What challenges still exist in your efforts to forgive yourself and others?

Prayer

"Way of the Cross," by Pope Francis

Loving Jesus,
you went up to Golgotha without hesitation, in utter love,
and let yourself be crucified without complaint.

Lowly Son of Mary,
you shouldered the burden of our night
to show us the immense light
with which you wanted to fill our hearts.
In your suffering is our redemption;
in your tears we see "the hour"
when God's gracious love is revealed.
In your final breath, as a man among men,
you lead us back, seven times forgiven,
to the heart of the Father,
and you show us, in your last words,
the path to the redemption of all our sorrows.
You, the Incarnate All, empty yourself on the cross,
understood only by her, your Mother,
who stood faithfully beneath that gibbet.
Your thirst is a wellspring of hope,
a hand extended even to the repentant thief,
who this day, thanks to you, enters paradise.
To all of us, crucified Lord Jesus,
grant your infinite mercy,
a fragrance of Bethany upon the world,
a cry of life for all humanity.
And at last, as we commend ourselves into the hands of your Father,
open unto us the doors of undying Life!
Amen.

Putting the Steps into Action

This is where the real work of recovery takes place. Complete the following before moving on to section 16:

☐ Make amends (with the direction of your sponsor)

When initiating contact with individuals on your list, be clear about the reason you want to approach them and ask for a time to meet. For those you cannot meet in person, schedule a phone call, an online meeting, or draft a letter to mail. Go forth with a spirit of humility and justice (focusing only on sweeping your side of the street) to make amends with those on your list. Move on to the next section once your sponsor and/or small workbook group discern that you have made adequate progress. You will continue to complete making your amends while progressing through the rest of this workbook and perhaps for the rest of your life if new opportunities arise.

Part III

THE EUCHARIST

STEP 10

Continued to take personal inventory and when we were wrong promptly admitted it.

SECTION 16

DAILY BREAD

Love is patient, love is kind. It is not jealous, [love] is not pompous, it is not inflated, it is not rude, it does not seek its own interests, it is not quick-tempered, it does not brood over injury, it does not rejoice over wrongdoing but rejoices with the truth. It bears all things, believes all things, hopes all things, endures all things.

—1 Corinthians 13:4–7

Exploration and Understanding

In Step 10, we continue the process of taking moral inventory and promptly admitting our wrongs. This is an ongoing Step—one that never ends. It's an expression of our continual call to Christian conversion. In the Catholic tradition, it's quite similar to making a daily examination of conscience to discern how we have responded to grace throughout our day. Completing a personal moral inventory on a regular basis—ideally, every day—offers a number of gifts, including the following:

- Forming a structure of accountability to God, ourselves, and others.
- Giving us permission to let go of the past and live in the present.
- Enabling us to both learn from our errors and recognize progress in both big and small ways.
- Helping us remain ever aware of how God is working in our lives—keeping us in a state of "God-consciousness."

By making a daily moral inventory, we not only become aware of our continuous need for grace but open up our hearts to receive the daily bread of God's mercy and love.

As Catholics, one way of receiving this daily bread is through the Eucharist. While the Lord pours out his grace in all sorts of ways, it's in the Eucharist that we find the source and summit of our Catholic faith. The Eucharist is a divine gift of thanksgiving: "The Eucharist is a sacrifice of thanksgiving to the Father, a blessing by which the Church expresses her gratitude to God for all his benefits, for all that he has accomplished through creation, redemption, and sanctification. Eucharist means first of all 'thanksgiving'" (CCC 1360).

Around the year 155, St. Justin Martyr beautifully captured the prayer of thanksgiving that takes place during the consecration of bread and wine: "Then someone brings bread and a cup of water and wine mixed together to him who presides over the brethren. He takes them and offers praise and glory to the Father of the universe, through the name of the Son and of the Holy Spirit and for a considerable time he gives thanks (in Greek: *eucharistian*) that we have been judged worthy of these gifts. When he has concluded the prayers and thanksgivings, all present give voice to an acclamation by saying: 'Amen.'"

When we receive the Eucharist with gratitude and trust in the Lord's mercy, we allow Jesus to transform our hearts. We can also receive healing and grace from simply being present before the Lord in Eucharistic Adoration. St. John Vianney advises, "When we are before the Blessed Sacrament, instead of looking about us, let us shut our eyes and open our hearts. . . . What delight we find in forgetting ourselves that we may seek God."

Let's not underestimate the power of gazing upon the Lord in the Eucharist. Aaron experienced the gift of the Eucharist during his recovery. For years, Aaron denied he had an addiction to pornography and believed he was capable of controlling his behavior. "Downloading porn videos and images as well as participating in sex chats—all are obvious markers of addiction. And I did them all," Aaron said.

This addiction played a role in the destruction of his marriage. And in the midst of that enormous crisis, things only became worse: "I was using pornography as self-medication for anxiety, depression, and loneliness following betrayal and heartbreak."

Eventually, by the grace of God, Aaron accepted that his life had become unmanageable and began his recovery. That same year, he started spending an hour in Eucharistic Adoration once a week. It was hard at first, and nothing "happened" right away. But as he kept going and started to listen to the Lord in silence, something began to change.

"I first talked and screamed and cried to our Lord during that hour. Finally, I listened. Kneeling before the Blessed Sacrament became for me the best therapy to recover from my addiction," Aaron shared. "I discovered the roots of my addiction in my personal therapy session with our Lord, who waited for me to repent when I strayed. Jesus in the Eucharist taught me about holiness, masculinity, and freedom from pornography. This helped me embrace the Steps I needed to take in my sobriety. The Lord's patience with me showed me that I needed to be vulnerable by asking for forgiveness from those whom I had hurt."

Aaron received the bread of forgiveness, courage, and healing from the Lord, transforming his heart and life. The Eucharist helped free him from the addictive scourge of pornography and masturbation.

Should I receive the Precious Blood at Mass if I'm a recovering alcoholic? The answer to this question will depend on the person and should be discussed with your sponsor. It's important to clarify that we do not miss out on anything by not receiving the Precious Blood since in the host we receive Christ's body, blood, soul, and divinity completely and fully. While there is no hard-and-fast rule, someone with a history of alcoholism may find it best to abstain from the Precious Blood to avoid unnecessary temptation.

Conducting a Daily Inventory

We commit to doing a daily inventory because this is how we hear the Lord speaking to us, encouraging us, and helping us grow in holiness and in our recovery. It's through conducting a daily inventory, by disposing ourselves to receive this daily bread, that we invite the Lord to help us see how we've loved and how we haven't. And then, in promptly admitting our faults to the Lord and to those we've offended, we ask for forgiveness and the strength to do better.

Here are a few questions to help us conduct our daily inventory:

- At what point during the day did my actions and intentions reflect my love for God with all my heart, mind, and soul?
- When did my actions and intentions fail to express love for God?
- How did my behavior show love for my neighbor as I wish to be loved?
- When did I come up short?

We can also turn to scripture as a model, specifically calling to mind St. Paul's wonderful definition of Christian love: "Love is patient, love is kind. It is not jealous, [love] is not pompous, it is not inflated, it is not rude, it does not seek its own interests, it is not quick-tempered, it does not brood over injury, it does not rejoice over wrongdoing but rejoices with the truth. It bears all things, believes all things, hopes all things, endures all things" (1 Cor 13:4–7).

In light of this scriptural passage, we might ask ourselves the following:

- Was I patient?
- Was I kind?
- Was I jealous?
- Was I pompous?
- Did I inflate the truth?
- Was I rude?
- Was I seeking my own interests?
- Was I quick-tempered?
- Did I brood over injury?
- Did I rejoice over wrongdoing?
- Did I rejoice with the truth?
- Did I bear all that was given to me?
- Did I maintain belief?
- Did I share hope?
- Did I endure in the face of difficulty?

There are countless ways to conduct a daily moral inventory. Doing so after the reception of the Eucharist or during Eucharistic Adoration can be especially powerful. When we conduct our moral inventory, we need to invite the Lord to show us where we have fallen short as well as where we have acted with love. Authentic humility requires us to be honest about our successes as well as our failures. The more we do this, the more the Lord can give us our "daily bread" and lead us on our spiritual and recovery journeys.

Recovery Tool

When taking personal inventory, we aim to balance our assets with our liabilities, our strengths with our weaknesses, and our successes with our failures.

Recovery Tool

By regularly using a gratitude journal to write down what we're thankful for and how we can share gratitude with others, we can foster a habit of thankfulness.

Reflection Questions

Take time to think about and write down responses to the following questions. Once you've done so, discuss your responses with your sponsor and/or small workbook group.

- How do you maintain a daily inventory and a God-consciousness in your life?
- What tools and practices help calibrate your spirit on a daily basis?
- How does the Sacrament of the Eucharist influence your recovery journey and spiritual life? Please share from personal experience.

Prayer
Prayer from the Breastplate of St. Patrick

I arise today
Through the strength of heaven;
Light of the sun,
Splendor of fire,
Speed of lightning,
Swiftness of the wind,
Depth of the sea,
Stability of the earth,
Firmness of the rock.

I arise today
Through God's strength to pilot me;
God's might to uphold me,
God's wisdom to guide me,
God's eye to look before me,
God's ear to hear me,
God's word to speak for me,
God's hand to guard me,
God's way to lie before me,
God's shield to protect me,
God's hosts to save me
Afar and anear,
Alone or in a multitude.
Christ shield me today
Against wounding
Christ with me, Christ before me, Christ behind me,
Christ in me, Christ beneath me, Christ above me,
Christ on my right, Christ on my left,
Christ when I lie down, Christ when I sit down,
Christ in the heart of everyone who thinks of me,
Christ in the mouth of everyone who speaks of me,
Christ in the eye that sees me,
Christ in the ear that hears me.
I arise today
Through the mighty strength
Of the Lord of creation.
Amen.

Putting the Steps into Action

This is where the real work of recovery takes place. Complete the following before moving on to section 17:

☐ Begin to practice a daily moral inventory

 Your daily personal inventory should become a permanent practice that sustains your spiritual progress. Seek regular encounters with Jesus in the Eucharist through Mass and Eucharistic Adoration.

STEP 11

Sought through prayer and meditation to improve our conscious contact with God as we understood Him, praying only for knowledge of His will for us and the power to carry that out.

SECTION 17

PRAYER AND MEDITATION

Finally, brothers, whatever is true, whatever is honorable, whatever is just, whatever is pure, whatever is lovely, whatever is gracious, if there is any excellence and if there is anything worthy of praise, think about these things.

—Philippians 4:8

Exploration and Understanding

As with Step 10, we never really finish Step 11—it is an ongoing part of our recovery and spiritual lives. Constant prayer and meditation are how we remain close to the Lord, continue to hear his voice, and learn to become more like him.

Twelve Steps and Twelve Traditions reminds us that prayer is as vital to our health as air, food, and sunshine. "As the body can fail its purpose for lack of nourishment, so can the soul. We all need the light of God's reality, the nourishment of his strength, and the atmosphere of his grace" (pp. 97–98).

The Catholic spiritual master St. Francis de Sales offers us a roadmap to the spiritual life in his luminous *Introduction to the Devout Life*. The great saint reminds us over and over again of the power of continued prayer: "Inasmuch as prayer places our understanding in the clearness of divine light, and exposes our will to the warmth of heavenly love, there is nothing which so purges our understanding of its ignorance and our will of its depraved inclinations; it is the water of benediction, which, when our souls are watered therewith, makes the plants of our good desires revive and flourish, cleanses our souls of their imperfections, and quenches the thirst caused by the passions of our hearts" (p. 75).

St. Francis de Sales also gives us a wonderful model of prayerfully meditating on our Lord so as to become more like him. "But above all I recommend to you prayer of the mind and heart and especially that which has for its subject the life and passion of our Lord; for by beholding him often in meditation, your whole soul will form your actions after the model of his. . . . By keeping close to the Saviour in meditation, and observing his words, his actions, and his affections, [we] shall learn, with the help of his grace, to speak, to act, and to will like him" (p. 75).

135

Acknowledging the necessity of maintaining constant and conscious contact with God, we next ask, what are some ways of doing so? Our rich Catholic tradition offers us numerous ways to pray and meditate: "The Lord leads all persons by paths and in ways pleasing to him, and each believer responds according to his heart's resolve and the personal expressions of his prayer. However, Christian Tradition has retained three major expressions of prayer: vocal, meditative, and contemplative. They have one basic trait in common: composure of heart. This vigilance in keeping the Word and dwelling in the presence of God makes these three expressions intense times in the life of prayer" (CCC 2699).

Common vocal prayers include the Our Father, Glory Be, and Hail Mary. When we participate in the liturgy of the Mass, we utter beautiful prayers to God the Father that have been handed down to us over many centuries. Of course, we can also offer up our own vocal prayers, speaking to the Lord from the heart as we would to a loved one and intimate friend.

Further, we can engage in the many rich forms of meditative prayer. The Rosary is one of the most well-known expressions of meditative prayer, inviting us to ponder the mysteries of Christ's life. Another way to meditate is to imagine ourselves in the stories of the gospels or to reflect deeply on a key phrase, word, or insight we find there. We can also follow the ancient practice of meditating on scripture known as lectio divina.

Finally, we can rest quietly with the Lord in contemplative prayer. We may do so by interiorly repeating a simple prayer over and over again to calm our minds and hearts, such as "Jesus, I trust in you," "Come, Holy Spirit," or "Lord Jesus Christ, Son of God, have mercy on me a sinner," until the words fall away and we're left only gazing at the Lord in the chamber of our hearts. As the *Catechism of the Catholic Church* informs us, "Contemplative prayer is the simple expression of the mystery of prayer. It is a gaze of faith fixed on Jesus, an attentiveness to the Word of God, a silent love" (2724).

In the Step 11 Faith in Action Activity on page 139, we list many ways to develop and maintain a vibrant prayer life. Some of the ways detailed on the handout include the following:

- Attending daily Mass.
- Committing to a Holy Hour every week.
- Receiving the Sacrament of Reconciliation once a month.
- Reading and meditating on scripture regularly.
- Praying the Liturgy of the Hours throughout the day.
- Repeating and meditating on the short prayer "Lord Jesus Christ, Son of God, have mercy on me a sinner" throughout the day.
- Prayerfully reflecting on the daily Mass readings.
- Reciting a daily Rosary or Chaplet of Divine Mercy.
- Doing spiritual journaling.
- Reciting an intercessory novena to a saint.

The suggestions above and others listed in the Step 11 handout only scratch the surface—there are many, many ways to deepen our prayer lives.

You may find that some practices resonate more deeply with you than others. You may also discover that in certain seasons of life you're drawn to some forms of prayer and meditation that haven't attracted you before. What matters most is that we're connecting with the Lord every day through prayer so that we can hear his voice and become more like him. St. Thérèse of Lisieux wrote, "For me prayer is a surge of the heart, it is a simple look towards Heaven, it is a cry of recognition and of love, embracing both trial and joy."

The Power of Devotional Prayer

In October 2014, Charlie looked at porn for the last time. "In my customary shame and regret I went on a frantic search for a cure—as had become my habit. This moment in time coincided with my conversion to the Catholic Church from the Calvinist wings of Protestantism. It was on this day in particular that I read about the power of the Rosary and the miracles wrought by Our Lady in the lives of so many through this form of prayer. As a meager act of faith, I decided to take Mary up on her offer," Charlie shared.

Although Charlie was skeptical, he was hopeful. He dedicated himself to praying the Rosary on his knees every day to overcome his pornography use. Whenever he got the urge to look at porn, he would drop to his knees and turn to the Blessed Mother.

"The Rosary is such a good antidote for me because it draws my mind out of the addiction and into Christ. I think that Mary holds this devotion out to us as a powerful weapon against our sins and addictions because it is her primary mission to lead souls to her son, Jesus," Charlie said.

By the grace of God, this incredible spiritual weapon—the Holy Rosary—lifted Charlie from the scourge of his addiction. It's a potent reminder of the sheer power of prayer, and why it remains the lifeblood of our spiritual life and recovery.

Recovery Tool

Prayer is not our attempt to bend God's will toward ours. Rather, prayer helps us to bend our will toward the Lord's.

Reflection Questions

Take time to think about and write down responses to the following questions. Once you've done so, discuss your responses with your sponsor and/or small workbook group.

- How do you practice prayer and meditation as recommended in Step 11?
- What are the fruits of your regular prayer and meditation practices?

- What activities and routines help you maintain conscious contact with God?

Prayer

Prayer of St. Francis

Lord,
Make me an instrument of your peace.
Where there is hatred, let me bring love.
Where there is injury, pardon.
Where there is doubt, faith.
Where there is despair, hope.
Where there is darkness, light.
Where there is sadness, joy.
Where there is discord, harmony.
Where there is error, truth.
Where there is wrong, the spirit of forgiveness.
O Divine Master,
Grant that I may not so much seek
to be consoled as to console,
to be understood as to understand,
to be loved as to love.
For it is in giving that we receive,
it is in pardoning that we are pardoned,
and it is in dying that we are born to eternal life.
Amen.

Putting the Steps into Action

This is where the real work of recovery takes place. Complete the following exercise before moving on to section 18:

☐ Faith in Action Activity

> Do not be afraid to experiment with new ideas and to alter your routine as time passes. As you continue to work Step 11, your relationship with God will develop and evolve. Thus, your daily practice is likely to vary over time to reflect this growth.

Faith in Action Activity

> **Step 11:** Sought through prayer and meditation to improve our conscious contact with God as we understood Him, praying only for knowledge of His will for us and the power to carry that out.

In Step 11, we develop a daily routine that deepens our relationship with the Lord and leads us on the path toward wholeness. Everyone's relationship with Christ is unique and, as such, may incorporate more or less of various elements of worship. For example, some people may go to daily Mass but only spend time in Eucharistic Adoration once every so often. This Step is about coming to radically accept God's will for us and to make knowledge of his will and power to carry that out our primary concern. Reflect on the following list and integrate three practices into your spiritual routine:

- Start attending daily Mass.
- Read and reflect on the daily Mass readings in your *Magnificat*, *Word Among Us*, at usccb.org, or on the Laudate app.
- Commit to spending one Holy Hour per week with the Lord.
- Pray the Liturgy of the Hours throughout the day, using the Hallow app.
- Receive the Sacrament of Reconciliation monthly.
- Read and meditate on scripture regularly.
- Repeat and meditate on the short prayer "Lord Jesus Christ, Son of God, have mercy on me a sinner" throughout the day.
- Do spiritual journaling.
- Join a local Bible study or prayer group that interests you.
- Make the Total Consecration to Jesus Christ through Mary.
- Be of service at your parish as a volunteer based on your gifts and talents.
- Pray the Rosary or Chaplet of Divine Mercy.
- Make a rosary or learn how to tie prayer knots.
- Read a book about a saint who resonates with you.
- Recite an intercessory novena to a saint.
- Go on a pilgrimage.
- Attend Eucharistic Adoration at a church you've never visited before.
- Consume only technology that inspires holiness. This applies to websites, music, movies, and TV.
- Meet with your spiritual director, sponsor, or faith mentor on a regular basis.

SECTION 18
SPIRITUAL AWARENESS

> And I will ask the Father, and he will give you another Advocate to be with you always, the Spirit of truth, which the world cannot accept, because it neither sees nor knows it. But you know it, because it remains with you, and will be in you.
>
> —John 14:16–17

Exploration and Understanding

Staying close to the Lord requires us to continually seek awareness of God's presence in our lives. This means regularly "checking in" with God through prayer and meditation to acknowledge when we have responded to the Holy Spirit's promptings and when we haven't. We can only do this by adopting a daily and intentional spiritual routine. Fortunately, there are many ways to maintain our daily awareness of God. Some of these spiritual routines and practices are detailed in the Step 11 Faith in Action Activity.

It's important to note that our emotions and moods play into our spiritual well-being. They may point to an area of our lives that we need to offer to the Lord. For example, feelings of anger or resentment may indicate that we need to ask the Lord for the grace of a forgiving heart, while feelings of peace and joy may indicate that the Lord is calling us toward a particular path. By being aware of our emotions and feelings, we're able to better invite the Lord into our lives through prayer and meditation.

One way of keeping track of our interior lives is to journal and reflect on our thoughts and feelings. Every evening we can write down what we're experiencing and imagine God responding to our concerns, joys, emotions, thoughts, and fears. As we journal, we might invite the Lord to provide us with clarity and peace, to reveal some new insight, or to accept our current interior state and offer it up to him.

The more we do this, the more we'll develop a better understanding of what's going on in our hearts. We'll be able to monitor our emotions and examine their causes. Being aware of our emotions also enables us to develop the practice of acceptance. Acceptance that where we are today is exactly where the Lord wants us. Acceptance that we are loved by God no matter what we think or feel in a given moment. A popular story from the back of the Big Book highlights the importance of acceptance:

Acceptance is the answer to all my problems today. When I am disturbed, it is because I find some person, place, thing, or situation—some fact of my life—unacceptable to me, and I can find no serenity until I accept that person, place, thing, or situation as being exactly the way it is supposed to be at this moment. Nothing, absolutely nothing, happens in God's world by mistake. Until I could accept my alcoholism, I could not stay sober; unless I accept life completely on life's terms, I cannot be happy. (*Alcoholics Anonymous*, p. 417)

Today, Trevor maintains conscious contact with God through a disciplined life of prayer and meditation. But this wasn't always the case. Drinking made up much of his adult life, which was an eventful one. He lived in Okinawa while serving in the US Navy, spent time in a Jesuit novitiate before being dismissed, and lived for ten years in New York City immersed in the music scene as a drummer. "Through it all, I didn't deny I was an alcoholic. I just didn't care," he recalled.

Trevor was in and out of rehab and managed to endure seasons of sobriety and attend AA meetings. After maintaining sobriety for three years and starting a nonprofit called Warrior Beat that promotes healing, well-being, fellowship, and reintegration for military veterans through facilitated group drumming, Trevor found that things were getting better. But something was still missing from his life.

"In 2019, I had been sober for three years, but God was not really a part of my recovery program. I ended up relapsing and getting my third DUI, which required extensive jail time," Trevor shared. When he got out of jail, he finally surrendered.

"I remember sitting on my back porch and I started to pray. I said, 'I can't do this without you and I need your guidance,' and it was the first time I had an overwhelming spiritual experience. I felt the presence of Christ with me at that moment urging me to come back to the faith. I received the Sacrament of Reconciliation for the first time in fifteen years and then received the Eucharist. I felt that my obsession with drinking was lifted. When I surrendered and allowed God to enter my heart, it was just gone," Trevor said.

Trevor's higher power became Jesus Christ. His recovery now incorporates the sacraments, prayer, meditation, and the company of fellow Catholics. "Choosing Christ is an action statement, and choosing Christ as a higher power is to respond to the grace that God has given me. To live as Christ commanded requires being connected to the Bride of Christ, the Church. I started a devotion to our Blessed Mother and a strong daily routine centered around prayer. Living the Catholic moral life requires discipline and prayer and making reception of the Eucharist a priority," Trevor said.

Meditation is also a major piece of Trevor's routine of maintaining spiritual awareness. He shares this:

> I teach meditation to veterans and lead meditations during Catholic in Recovery meetings. Meditation is a unique way that we encounter God. As we read in the Big Book, we are called to seek prayer and meditation to improve our conscious contact

with God, and so prayer and meditation are different things. To me, prayer is more conversational, where we are giving thanks to God and asking for guidance and inspiration. Meditation is the act of just being with God and the Holy Spirit in the present moment. It's communicating to the Lord that I love you so much that I'm just going to sit here and enjoy your presence and grace. It's the ultimate sign that we trust that God is directing our lives when we can stop our wandering and scheming minds, and turn our will and lives over to God and simply be present.

The Spiritual Exercises of St. Ignatius

The Spiritual Exercises are a compilation of meditations, prayers, and contemplative practices developed by St. Ignatius of Loyola to help us deepen our awareness of God's voice. Originally, the exercises were worked through over a thirty-day retreat of solitude and silence. Today, the exercises have been adapted so that laypeople can complete them while meeting their daily responsibilities (and without needing to go on a month-long retreat). They can be used to help us maintain our conscious contact with God and discern the Lord's will in our daily lives.

In fact, the Spiritual Exercises have much in common with the Twelve Steps. Jim Harbaugh, SJ, details the overlap in his engaging book *A 12-Step Approach to the Spiritual Exercises of St. Ignatius.* If we have worked through the Twelve Steps, integrating the Spiritual Exercises can be a wonderful way to deepen our spiritual awareness:

> A lot of recovering people may find that the spiritual path they have begun with the Twelve Steps leads to other, sometimes surprising paths—any self-respecting spiritual path ought to. It may even lead them to want to explore the path Ignatius stumbled on almost five hundred years ago. Some of the scenery will seem decidedly familiar. In the same way, people who have made the Spiritual Exercises may subsequently find they need the Twelve Steps. They too may feel curiously at home in the world of the Recovering. (p. xviii)

Similar to the Twelve Steps, actively working through the Ignatian Spiritual Exercises can offer a number of spiritual fruits:

- Consolation
- Closeness to God
- Self-awareness
- Freedom from shame and pride
- An attitude of exploration
- Recognition of both one's sin and one's usefulness to God
- Knowledge of Jesus
- Knowledge of self
- Discernment
- Love of God

Ultimately, incorporating the Spiritual Exercises can be a powerful, enriching way of maintaining our conscious contact with God and deepening our daily routine of prayer and meditation.

Recovery Tool

Not only do the Twelve Steps have the power to help save our lives, but they also give us a guide for living our lives.

Recovery Tool

Accepting a situation is not the same as approving of it.

Reflection Questions

Take time to think about and write down responses to the following questions. Once you've done so, discuss your responses with your sponsor and/or small workbook group.

- What consistent spiritual practices help you know and do the will of God?
- What tools are helpful as you check in with yourself throughout the day?
- Discuss your experience and/or questions around the Spiritual Exercises of St. Ignatius.

Prayer

"Suscipe," by St. Ignatius Loyola

Take, Lord, and receive all my liberty,
my memory, my understanding,
and my entire will,
all I have and call my own.
You have given all to me.
To you, Lord, I return it.
Everything is yours; do with it what you will.
Give me only your love and your grace,
that is enough for me.
Amen.

Putting the Steps into Action

This is where the real work of recovery takes place. Complete the following before moving on to section 19:

☐ Discuss your experience with Steps 10 and 11 and share about a few newly adopted spiritual practices with your sponsor and/or small workbook group

 Visit the digital platform at www.catholicinrecovery.com/cirworkbook to watch video testimonies and read stories about how others have integrated new routines and practices to enlarge their spiritual lives and recovery.

Putting the Steps into Action

This is where the real work of recovery takes place. Complete the following before moving on to section 19.

☐ Discuss your experience with Steps 10 and 11 and share about a few newly adopted spiritual practices with your sponsor and/or small-workbook group

☐ Visit the digital platform at www.catholicinrecovery.com/airworkbook to watch video testimonies and read stories about how others have integrated new routines and practices to enlarge their spiritual lives and recovery.

Part IV
CONFIRMATION

STEP 12

*Having had a spiritual awakening
as a result of these Steps,
we tried to carry this message
to others, and to practice these
principles in all our affairs.*

SECTION 19

SERVICE

Amen, I say to you, whatever you did for one of these least brothers of mine, you did for me.

—Matthew 25:40

Exploration and Understanding

Step 12 encourages us to give to others what we've received. For Catholics, both Confirmation, which seals the covenant of Baptism, and the spiritual awakening we've found as a result of working the Twelve Steps call for self-sacrifice and service to others. We've come to know the power of Christ through the gift of the Steps and the sacraments—now we must share the Good News with others. As St. James tells us, "If anyone among you should stray from the truth and someone bring him back, he should know that whoever brings back a sinner from the error of his way will save his soul from death and will cover a multitude of sins" (5:19–20).

Jenny was able to quit smoking—even meth—without a recovery program. But when it came to drinking, she couldn't stop: "I wondered what it was about alcohol that I couldn't give up." She drank for many years in secret, her husband and two daughters having no idea about her addiction. While living as a high-functioning alcoholic, she eventually went back to the Catholic Church when her father returned to it. Soon after, she had a powerful experience in the Sacrament of Reconciliation and began working on her relationship with Christ. She also began serving in her parish as a Eucharistic minister and lector. This brought her in contact with Catholic in Recovery, where she met other Catholics involved in AA and NA and was exposed to the Twelve Steps.

Despite attending Catholic in Recovery meetings, Jenny was still drinking daily—and lying about it. She recalled, "I would always save enough alcohol to have some the following morning. I was miserable, and during a night of not being able to fall asleep, I began praying the first three Steps over and over again—admitting that I'm powerless, that my life was unmanageable, and that only God can save me. I cried, and I never prayed harder in my life. Somehow, I woke up the next morning and poured out the alcohol I had saved for myself."

As a result, Jenny became very sick physically as she experienced withdrawals. Her husband and daughters were alarmed and confused by her sudden illness. A couple of days later, still intensely ill, she admitted to her husband what had been going on. "I told him the reason I was so sick was that I'd been secretly drinking for years and that I needed help. I also texted the men at Catholic in Recovery and revealed that I had been lying to them about not drinking and that I might not be married anymore since I had just told my husband the truth."

But her husband responded by giving her a hug and then invited her to tell their daughters the truth as well. Afterward, she entered an outpatient program and stopped drinking for good.

As we highlighted in section 6 of this workbook, there are many ways we can be merciful to others and bring others back to God, our loving Father. The Church details both corporal (or bodily) and spiritual works of mercy that we can adopt. Spiritual works of mercy, such as counseling the doubtful or instructing the ignorant, take place when we offer support to fellow addicts by sharing experience, strength, and hope. Our service can extend to others through tangible corporal works of mercy. Here they are again:

Corporal Works of Mercy	**Spiritual Works of Mercy**
• Feed the hungry	• Counsel the doubtful
• Give drink to the thirsty	• Instruct the ignorant
• Shelter the homeless	• Admonish the sinner
• Visit the sick	• Comfort the sorrowful
• Visit the imprisoned	• Forgive injuries
• Bury the dead	• Bear wrongs patiently
• Give alms to the poor	• Pray for the living and the dead

When we share the good news of our recovery and our love of Christ with others, we are sustained and helped in our own recovery. Loving others allows us to love ourselves, and vice versa. We read in the Big Book that "nothing will so much insure immunity from drinking as intensive work with other alcoholics. . . . This is our twelfth suggestion: Carry this message to other alcoholics! You can help when no one else can. You can secure their confidence when others fail" (*Alcoholics Anonymous*, p. 89).

But the fruits of helping others maintain recovery are not limited to simply keeping ourselves in recovery. Rather, our life becomes immeasurably richer. We start to understand what Christ meant when he said the kingdom of heaven is upon us, as the more we serve others in love, the more we experience the joy and peace of his kingdom. In other words, we realize for ourselves how right the Big Book is: "Life will take on new meaning. To watch people recover, to see them help others, to watch loneliness vanish, to see a fellowship grow up about you, to have a host of friends—this is an experience you must not miss" (*Alcoholics Anonymous*, p. 89).

While Jenny's husband and daughters were supportive of her recovery, they still harbored anger and confusion. She knew saying sorry wouldn't be enough—that she would have to show them, over time, that she was serious about recovery. Eventually, they began to see that her change was for real and God was transforming her.

"My husband doesn't practice his faith, but he recently told me that listening to me pray is very peaceful. And my younger daughter came to me last year and shared that she was having intrusive thoughts, and I was able to help her and be there for her," Jenny said. Jenny became an example of vulnerability, honesty, love, and service to her family and others in her life. In other words, she continues to live out Step 12.

"I'm open about being in recovery on social media as well as professionally and personally. And people have come up to me and asked, 'How do I know if I have a problem with drinking?' And this gives me the chance to share the good news of recovery and God's grace," Jenny said. "I get to tell them that, even if they don't feel that God can help them, they can borrow a little bit of my faith to help allow God to bring recovery and healing to their own lives."

Let's end this section with some valuable tips that *Alcoholics Anonymous* offers in working an ongoing Step 12 and helping others struggling with addiction.

- "If he does not want to stop drinking, don't waste time trying to persuade him. You may spoil a later opportunity. This advice is given for his family also. They should be patient, realizing they are dealing with a sick person" (p. 90).
- "Tell him enough about your drinking (thinking) habits, symptoms, and experiences to encourage him to speak of himself" (p. 91).
- "Tell him how baffled you were, how you finally learned that you were sick. Give him an account of the struggles you made to stop" (p. 92).
- "Insist that if he is severely afflicted, there may be little chance he can recover by himself" (p. 92).
- "Continue to speak of [addiction] as an illness, a fatal malady. Talk about the conditions of body and mind which accompany it. Keep his attention focused mainly on your personal experience" (p. 92).
- "Stress the spiritual feature freely. If the man be agnostic or atheist, make it emphatic that he does not have to agree with your conception of God" (p. 93).
- "To be vital, faith must be accompanied by self-sacrifice and unselfish, constructive action" (p. 93).

Recovery Tool

Never underestimate your ability to help another person impacted by addiction.

Recovery Tool

We get out of ourselves by serving others—and this paradoxically enables us to be fully ourselves.

Reflection Questions

Take time to think about and write down responses to the following questions. Once you've done so, discuss your responses with your sponsor and/or small workbook group.

- What service opportunities are there in your local community or elsewhere to help others? How about those specifically suffering from an addiction?
- How has working with and/or serving others strengthened your recovery?
- How have you been enriched by others who have served you?

Prayer

Prayer of St. Teresa of Avila

Govern everything by your wisdom, O Lord,
so that my soul may always be serving you in the way you will
and not as I choose.
Let me die to myself so that I may serve you;
let me live to you who are life itself.
Amen.

Putting the Steps into Action

This is where the real work of recovery takes place. Complete the following before moving on to section 20:

☐ Take on a service commitment at a Catholic in Recovery meeting or other type of recovery meeting within the next month

 Service commitments at meetings can take on many forms and may include assuming responsibility for one aspect of the meeting (hospitality, literature, or treasury), taking on a larger role (group secretary), or starting a new Catholic in Recovery group.

SECTION 20

MAKE DISCIPLES

The eleven disciples went to Galilee, to the mountain to which Jesus had ordered them. When they saw him, they worshiped, but they doubted. Then Jesus approached and said to them, "All power in heaven and on earth has been given to me. Go, therefore, and make disciples of all nations, baptizing them in the name of the Father, and of the Son, and of the holy Spirit, teaching them to observe all that I have commanded you. And behold, I am with you always, until the end of the age."

—Matthew 28:16–20

Exploration and Understanding

As Christians, we are marked by Christ's spirit. We are named one of his unique, unrepeatable disciples and called to make disciples of others, starting with those closest to us—our family members, friends, and those in our community. Recall that we are welcomed into Christ's family through Baptism, and that the Sacrament of Confirmation deepens our call to be disciples. We read in the *Catechism of the Catholic Church*: "Christ himself declared that he was marked with his Father's seal. Christians are also marked with a seal: 'It is God who establishes us with you in Christ and has commissioned us; he has put his seal on us and given us his Spirit in our hearts as a guarantee' (2 Cor 1:21–22). This seal of the Holy Spirit marks our total belonging to Christ, our enrollment in his service for ever, as well as the promise of divine protection in the great eschatological trial" (1296).

The grace offered us in the Sacrament of Confirmation is extraordinary. In fact, the *Catechism* explains how it increases and deepens our baptismal grace in certain key ways:

> It roots us more deeply in the divine filiation which makes us cry, "Abba! Father!"; it unites us more firmly to Christ; it increases the gifts of the Holy Spirit in us [wisdom, understanding, counsel, fortitude, knowledge, piety, and fear of the Lord]; it renders our bond with the Church more perfect; it gives us a special strength of the Holy Spirit to spread and defend the faith by word and action as true witnesses of Christ, to confess the name of Christ boldly, and never to be ashamed of the Cross. (1302)

153

Yet, to allow these gifts to be active in our lives, we need to dispose ourselves to them by regularly partaking in the Eucharist and the Sacrament of Reconciliation as well as practicing our recovery principles. These principles include honesty, humility, a willingness to acknowledge wrongdoing and promptly admit it to others, a commitment to service, maintaining conscious contact with God, and many others that we've covered in this workbook.

We also dispose ourselves to these gifts of the Holy Spirit by remaining part of a community—staying within the herd—and allowing ourselves to be known and loved by others so that we may do the same with them. Ernest Kurtz and Katherine Ketcham offer valuable insight on the importance of being part of a community in their book *The Spirituality of Imperfection: Storytelling and the Search for Meaning*:

> Rather than asking why we need community, it may be more important to ask how we need others. Wisdom's answer to that question, the answer embodied in the spirituality of imperfection, is that human beings need each other precisely in relationships of mutuality. Mutuality involves not just "give or get," nor even "give and get." In relationships of mutuality we give by getting and get by giving, recognizing that we truly gain only what we seek to give and that we are able to give only that which we are seeking to gain. (p. 83)

It's by remaining rooted in a community, living out the principles of recovery, and encountering Christ regularly through his sacraments that we live out Step 12. And when we do so, our life takes on a heavenly glow, allowing us to share our message of hope, healing, and mercy.

Jonathan craved affirmation ever since he was a boy. "I got so deep into needing this affirmation that I would often tell lies about how good I was at sports to try and get affirmation. Eventually, I would be discovered as a phony. But then I discovered drugs and alcohol, which offered me an escape to numb all of my pain."

Jonathan eventually rediscovered his Catholic faith and entered the rooms of recovery, finding sobriety, healing, and mercy. But then his life changed. He moved away, got engaged, and started graduate school. While he immediately got plugged into a local parish, he stopped attending recovery meetings.

"Suddenly, I was taking the inventory of others—rather than myself—and began using it as an excuse to stop being involved in recovery. Besides, I was busy and only had so many hours in the day, so I thought."

Jonathan became what he referred to as a "dry drunk"—someone sober but not active in recovery. As he neglected recovery, he stopped being able to relate to others. He met people at his parish who didn't understand his alcoholic past, and so he felt he couldn't be honest and open with them. "Although I was still doing service work during my dry drunk period, my service felt dead. Showing up at the soup kitchen became just another box to check to help get me into heaven."

Jonathan had lost his ability to see Christ in others because he was isolated from a recovery community—from a place of acceptance and love where he could lead with his weakness and woundedness to be known and loved as he was, allowing him to then know and love others in return. "A lot of people when they come into a 12-Step program think that they might 'graduate' once they get to Step 12. In reality, this is only the beginning of our recovery. I have found in the nine years I have been sober that the times I tend to stagnate spiritually are the times when I am isolated."

In time, Jonathan found his way back to recovery and regained his ability to encounter others with love and joy. This allowed him to once again share the good news of God's love as a beloved disciple. By remaining part of a recovery community, practicing his faith regularly, and continuing to work the Steps, he once again realized that his very wounds can invite others to the healing mercy of God. In this way we imitate Christ, who, when he comes upon his disciples afraid and uncertain, shows them the wounds of his glorified body to offer them peace and forgiveness.

"In order to be more Christlike, I needed to be more honest with myself, realize that these wounds are there and likely always will be, not allow them to have power over me, and then use them to call others to greater conversion. As recovering addicts, we get to experience this in a major way when we work Step 12 continuously in our lives," Jonathan said.

As Jonathan came to see, we never finish working Step 12, just as we never finish seeking to be more and more like Christ to those in our family, parish, and larger community: "Many people continue to serve others on their journey in recovery out of pure gratitude for the gift they have been given. We seek to wash one another's feet as Christ taught us. Nothing is more satisfying for someone in recovery than to help someone who is still sick and suffering."

Recovery Tool
St. Paul reminds us that when we are weak, we are strong. We lead with our weakness because in weakness there is unity with Christ, and in unity with Christ, victory.

Recovery Tool
An "I" program leads to "illness," but a "we" program leads to "wellness."

Reflection Questions

Take time to think about and write down responses to the following questions. Once you've done so, discuss your responses with your sponsor and/or small workbook group.

• How do you see your role as a disciple?

• Describe how you share a message of hope with others and practice spiritual principles in all your affairs.

• Reflecting on your experience using this workbook, please share primary takeaways or moments of clarity that will remain with you.

Prayer

Prayer of St. Augustine

Lord Jesus, let me know myself and know thee,
and desire nothing save only thee.
Let me hate myself and love thee.
Let me do everything for the sake of thee.
Let me humble myself and exalt thee.
Let me think nothing except thee.
Let me die to myself and live in thee.
Let me accept whatever happens as from thee.
Let me banish self and follow thee,
and ever desire to follow thee.
Let me fly from myself and take refuge in thee,
that I may deserve to be defended by thee.
Let me fear for myself, let me fear thee,
and let me be among those who are chosen by thee.
Let me distrust myself and put my trust in thee.
Let me be willing to obey for the sake of thee.
Let me cling to nothing save only to thee,
and let me be poor because of thee.
Look upon me, that I may love thee.
Call me that I may see thee,
and forever enjoy thee.
Amen.

Putting the Steps into Action

This is where the real work of recovery takes place. Complete the following before moving on to the concluding section:

☐ Be of service to others in your family, community, parish, or workplace

☐ Practice 12-Step principles in all areas of your life

 A gift as miraculous as recovery can only be kept if we are willing to give it away. Service can take on many forms, and we are all called to give back in various ways. The body of Christ has many parts which serve different purposes (see 1 Corinthians 12:12). Avoid making judgments about the form of service you or others are called to. Your talents, experiences, and charisms will be informative as you discern how you are called to serve.

Putting the Steps into Action

This is where the real work of recovery takes place. Complete the following before moving on to the concluding section:

☐ Be of service to others in your family, community, parish, or workplace

☐ Practice 12-Step principles in all areas of your life

A gift as miraculous as recovery can only be kept if we are willing to give it away. Service can take on many forms, and we are all called to give back in various ways. The body of Christ has many parts which serve different purposes (see 1 Corinthians 12:12). Avoid making judgments about the form of service you or others are called to. Your talents, experiences, and other gifts will be informative as you discern how you are called to serve.

CONTINUING OUR JOURNEY OF RECOVERY

Congratulations, you have reached the end of this workbook! Yet, while you've finished this small workbook journey over the last several weeks and months, our larger journey of recovery is one that never ends. Just as our participation in the Church's sacramental life, which begins with Baptism, is ongoing, we never stop living out the many life-giving principles of recovery and seeking to grow in love for God and neighbor. So, what does continuing our journey of recovery look like?

As we've mentioned throughout this workbook, it's *vital* that we remain connected to a recovery group. It's in the company of others that we both know and love others as well as become known and loved. It's in a community that we lead with our weaknesses to find unity and strength, that we offer hope to those without it, and that we come to see the face of Christ in others. We must remain connected to others who can keep us accountable, honest, and on the path of sobriety and holiness. We simply *cannot* maintain a healthy recovery without others.

Continuing our journey of recovery means intentionally fostering in our lives the principles detailed in this workbook. For example, as sinners in need of God's mercy, we *must* continue to take a personal moral inventory so that we can promptly admit our wrongdoing to others and seek forgiveness from God in the Sacrament of Reconciliation. The various inventory exercises provided in this workbook can offer a valuable ongoing resource in this regard.

You will find many opportunities to strengthen your recovery and deepen your relationship with Jesus Christ through the tools and learning modules offered on the Catholic in Recovery digital platform, as mentioned in the introduction. Even after many years of sobriety, there will remain areas of our lives that we haven't fully surrendered to God—areas where we're still trying to live life on our own terms, no matter how small or hidden. True holiness means surrendering *everything* to the Lord. Visit www.catholicinrecovery.com/cirworkbook to explore additional healing resources for individuals and families seeking freedom from addiction, including a series on sponsorship, worksheets and exercises focused on specific addiction types, and new content from the Catholic in Recovery community.

As St. John of the Cross reminds us, "The soul that is attached to anything, however much good there may be in it, will not arrive at the liberty of divine union. For whether it be a strong wire rope or a slender and delicate thread that holds the bird, it matters not, if it really holds it fast; for until the cord be broken the bird cannot fly." By continuing to work the Steps and participate in the sacramental life of the Church, we can gradually sever the many "wire ropes" and "delicate threads" that keep us from soaring closer to God.

Of course, continuing our journey of recovery also means remaining safely tucked within the bosom of the Church's sacramental and communal life that we have been ushered into through the Sacrament of Baptism. It means receiving and adoring the Sacrament of the Eucharist as much as we can, acknowledging it is truly the bread of life that has come down from heaven: the very Body of our Lord and Savior, Jesus Christ. It means frequenting the Sacrament of Reconciliation when we have fallen, knowing that our Father in heaven waits eagerly, like the father in the parable of the prodigal son, to run toward us, embrace us with joy, and prepare for us a splendid feast. And it means continuing to live out the call to bring Christ's healing and love to others, drawing on the charisms and gifts that the Holy Spirit has anointed us with through the Sacrament of Confirmation.

Finally, continuing our journey of recovery means fostering conscious contact with the One who loves us unconditionally: the triune God. Through the many treasures given to us by the Church—the Holy Rosary, the Liturgy of the Hours, the Divine Mercy chaplet, countless novenas and prayers to the saints, lectio divina, silent contemplation, and more—as well as our own intimate conversations with God, we are reminded that our most fundamental identity is that we are beloved children of God. From this place of belovedness, we cannot help but bring the good news of Christ's love for all to our families, recovery groups, parishes, communities, and the world.

Let's journey forward in our recovery with faith, hope, and love, knowing that the Lord Jesus walks alongside us, leading us from the darkness of addiction and sin to the eternal embrace of our loving Father in heaven!

> For I am convinced that neither death, nor life, nor angels, nor principalities, nor present things, nor future things, nor powers, nor height, nor depth, nor any other creature will be able to separate us from the love of God in Christ Jesus our Lord. (Romans 8:38–39)

RECOVERY TEAM ROSTER

Stay in the herd by forming and maintaining a connection to a community in recovery and at your parish. By doing so, you will find the strength and support that, with the aid of the Holy Spirit, can help you find healing through recovery. Use the template below to create a personalized Recovery Team Roster of people who are willing to walk with you in recovery.

	Name	Phone number	Email address
12-Step home group			
Sponsor			
Accountability partner			
Accountability partner			

	Name	Phone number	Email address
Accountability partner			
Confessor			
Spiritual director			
Therapist			
Mentor			
Mentor			
Mentor			

APPENDIX II

CATHOLIC IN RECOVERY MEETING RESOURCES
General Recovery Meeting Leader's Script

At the Beginning of the Meeting

Leader begins:

Welcome to our Catholic in Recovery meeting. This is a general recovery meeting that gathers every *[day(s) of the week]* at __:__ a.m./p.m. My name is _____.

The aim of these Catholic in Recovery meetings is to bring freedom to those struggling with addictions, compulsions, and unhealthy attachments. In addition, we are here to supplement one's personal recovery with a sacramental understanding of God's mercy using the traditions of the Catholic Church. We rely on our faithful understanding of Jesus Christ as our Savior and Higher Power, who, aided by the Holy Spirit, is accessible to us here and now. We hope you can find a personal relationship with Christ as you grow in this journey, regardless of where you are today.

To begin the meeting, we will unite in prayer. Please join me in reciting the Serenity Prayer. Let's begin in the name of the Father, and of the Son, and of the Holy Spirit:

> God,
> Grant me the serenity
> to accept the things I cannot change,
> the courage to change the things I can,
> and the wisdom to know the difference.
> Living one day at a time,
> enjoying one moment at a time,
> accepting hardship as the pathway to peace.
> Taking, as he did, this sinful world as it is, not as I would have it.
> Trusting that he will make all things right if I surrender to his will.
> That I may be reasonably happy in this life
> and supremely happy with him forever in the next.
> Amen.

The spiritual principles of these meetings are based on 12-Step recovery. I have asked _____ to read the Twelve Steps.

Turn your attention to this person and allow them to read the Twelve Steps (found on page 167).

Leader continues:

Next, please join me in reciting the Lord's Prayer:

> Our Father who art in heaven,
> hallowed be thy name.
> Thy kingdom come.
> Thy will be done on earth, as it is in heaven.
> Give us this day our daily bread,
> and forgive us our trespasses,
> as we forgive those who trespass against us,
> and lead us not into temptation,
> but deliver us from evil.
> For thine is the kingdom, the power, and the glory forever.
> Amen.

I have asked _____ to read our meeting guidelines.

Turn your attention to this person and allow them to read the Meeting Guidelines (found on page 169).

Leader continues:

Please introduce yourself in any way that you are comfortable, starting on my left. If you are here for the first time, please let us know.

Turn your attention to each group member as they introduce themselves.

Leader continues:

I will now turn the meeting over to the group secretary for any announcements and special occasions.

Turn your attention to the group secretary for announcements and to celebrate any recovery milestones.

Leader continues:

Three pillars that are crucial to recovery are honesty, openness, and willingness. While sharing your experience, strength, and hope with one another, please keep this in mind. Although it is often necessary to paint a picture of our situations, we are more concerned with the merciful solution offered by God's love. Thus, these meetings are dedicated not so much to dwelling on the past, but toward developing the appropriate attitudes and behavior for living this particular day successfully.

Using the materials in front of us, we will read through this week's meeting reflection. Each one ties together liturgical themes, scripture from Catholic Mass readings, and recovery principles. Each person can read a paragraph or two before passing to the next person, or feel free to pass altogether. When finished, I will begin sharing, then choose a direction to start our open discussion.

Turn your attention to the meeting reflection and take turns reading it before starting your opening share.

After the Discussion

Leader continues:

We will now send the meeting back to our secretary for some closing remarks and prayer . . .

feel free to pass altogether. When finished, I will begin sharing, then choose a direction to start our open discussion.

Turn your attention to the meeting reflection and take turns reading it before starting your opening share.

After the Discussion

We will now send the meeting back to our secretary for some closing remarks and prayer ...

The Twelve Steps

1. We admitted we were powerless over addictions, compulsions, and unhealthy attachments—that our lives had become unmanageable.
2. Came to believe that a Power greater than ourselves could restore us to sanity.
3. Made a decision to turn our will and our lives over to the care of God as we understood Him.
4. Made a searching and fearless moral inventory of ourselves.
5. Admitted to God, to ourselves, and to another human being the exact nature of our wrongs.
6. Were entirely ready to have God remove all these defects of character.
7. Humbly asked Him to remove our shortcomings.
8. Made a list of all persons we had harmed, and became willing to make amends to them all.
9. Made direct amends to such people wherever possible, except when to do so would injure them or others.
10. Continued to take personal inventory and when we were wrong promptly admitted it.
11. Sought through prayer and meditation to improve our conscious contact with God as we understood Him, praying only for knowledge of His will for us and the power to carry that out.
12. Having had a spiritual awakening as the result of these Steps, we tried to carry this message to others, and to practice these principles in all our affairs.

The Twelve Steps were reproduced and printed with permission from Alcoholics Anonymous World Services, Inc.

The Twelve Steps

1. We admitted we were powerless over addictions, compulsions, and unhealthy attachments—that our lives had become unmanageable.

2. Came to believe that a Power greater than ourselves could restore us to sanity.

3. Made a decision to turn our will and our lives over to the care of God as we understood

5. Admitted to God, to ourselves, and to another human being the exact nature of our

6. and removed all these defects of character.

7. our shortcomings.

8. and became willing to make amends to them

9. wherever possible, except when to do so would

Catholic in Recovery Meeting Guidelines

1. Please keep your sharing tied to your own experience, strength, and hope. Showing concern for another's difficulties is valuable, but claiming to have their solution or remarking about their situation on a group level can be counterproductive and prohibit further honesty. We are here to support one another, not fix each other.
2. Out of respect for the group as a whole, please limit your shares to a maximum of __ minutes. You will be alerted if you exceed that time.
3. Privacy within the group is critical. Anything that is said within the meeting should stay within the meeting. Rest assured that what is mentioned here will not make its way to others in the parish, the community, or elsewhere. This is all our responsibility.
4. Show respect for other people's differences. While our solution is generally the same, our experiences and understandings may be quite different. Thus, even religious differences ought to be respected.
5. You are invited to be as honest and open about your situation and experience as you are comfortable. The honest nature of these meetings brings us closer to Christ and one another.

Thank you in advance for respecting these guidelines!

Catholic in Recovery Meeting Guidelines

1. Please keep your sharing tied to your own experience, strength, and hope. Showing concern for another's difficulties is valuable, but claiming to have their solution or remarking about their situation on a group level can be counterproductive and prohibit further honesty. We are here to support one another, not fix each other.

... about your situation and experience as you ... these meetings brings us closer to Christ and one another.

Catholic in Recovery Meeting Secretary's Guide

Before the Meeting

- Set up room with appropriate number of chairs.
- Set out prayer sheets and meeting content before people arrive.
- Choose someone to lead the meeting (may have been determined beforehand or at end of last meeting):

    ◦ Give leader all three pages: Leader's Script, the Twelve Steps, and Meeting Guidelines.
    ◦ Suggest they ask someone to read the Twelve Steps and Meeting Guidelines.

- Determine if there are any announcements or celebrations for today's meeting.

At the Beginning of the Meeting

Leader will turn the meeting back to you for announcements and celebrations. Acknowledge them and say:

My name is _____ and I am your group secretary. Welcome, everyone, especially those here for the first time.

If there are any announcements, mention them here. Then continue:

We celebrate various lengths of recovery at 30, 60, and 90 days, 6 months, and every year of continuous sobriety, recovery, abstinence, clean time, or the like. We also celebrate those participating in the sacraments of the Church for the first time, or for the first time in a long time. If there are any upcoming celebrations, please let me know after the meeting. Today, I am aware of ___ special occasions. Is there anyone (else) celebrating a milestone?

If there are milestones, celebrate with tokens. Then, turn the meeting back to the leader.

At the End of the Meeting

Leader will return the meeting back to you. Say:

Let's thank _____ for leading a great meeting!

Recognize the leader one more time (however you'd like), congratulate special occasions, and welcome first-time members. Then, conclude:

Let's close in prayer. Please join me in reciting the St. Francis Prayer. We'll begin in the name of the Father, and of the Son, and of the Holy Spirit. . . ."

Pray the St. Francis Prayer on page 174.

Catholic in Recovery Meeting Secretary's Guide

Before the Meeting

- Set up room with appropriate number of chairs.
- Set out prayer sheets and meeting content before people arrive.
- Choose someone to lead the meeting (may have been determined beforehand or at end of last meeting).
  - _____ someone to lead the Twelve Steps and Meeting Guidelines.
- _____ if there are announcements or celebrations for today's meeting.

Beginning the Meeting

_____ announcements and celebrations. Acknowledge

_____ congratulate special occasions

APPENDIX III

CATHOLIC IN RECOVERY MEETING PRAYERS

Serenity Prayer

God,
Grant me the serenity
to accept the things I cannot change
the courage to change the things I can
and the wisdom to know the difference.
Living one day at a time,
enjoying one moment at a time,
accepting hardship as the pathway to peace.
Taking, as he did, this sinful world as it is,
not as I would have it.
Trusting that he will make all things right
if I surrender to his will.
That I may be reasonably happy in this life
and supremely happy with him forever in the next.
Amen.

Lord's Prayer

Our Father who art in heaven,
hallowed be thy name.
Thy kingdom come.
Thy will be done on earth, as it is in heaven.
Give us this day our daily bread,
and forgive us our trespasses,

as we forgive those who trespass against us,
and lead us not into temptation,
but deliver us from evil.
Amen.

St. Francis Prayer

Lord,
Make me an instrument of your peace.
Where there is hatred, let me bring love.
Where there is injury, pardon.
Where there is doubt, faith.
Where there is despair, hope.
Where there is darkness, light.
Where there is sadness, joy.
Where there is discord, harmony.
Where there is error, truth.
Where there is wrong, the spirit of forgiveness.
O Divine Master,
Grant that I may not so much seek
to be consoled as to console,
to be understood as to understand,
to be loved as to love.
For it is in giving that we receive,
it is in pardoning that we are pardoned,
and it is in dying that we are born to eternal life.
Amen.

APPENDIX IV

HOW TO FACILITATE A SMALL WORKBOOK GROUP

Catholic in Recovery community members report that working through the materials of this workbook with a small group is spiritually enriching, provides the necessary encouragement to complete the next exercise or step, and helps break through layers of denial that would otherwise prohibit honesty with themselves. After leading several small groups of individuals with a variety of addictions, compulsions, and unhealthy attachments through this workbook, we can offer several suggestions and notes on how you can organize a group to journey together through the Twelve Steps while integrating the sacraments of the Catholic Church.

First, there are a few things to consider before starting a group:

What

A Catholic in Recovery small workbook group is a gathering of men and women who meet regularly—typically weekly—to work through the Twelve Steps of addiction recovery following the outline and activities of this workbook. Between meetings, participants are encouraged to complete the exercises, worksheets, and activities suggested at the end of each section to make consistent progress. Adequate time is provided at the beginning of each small workbook group meeting for members to check in with each other and share their findings. On average, small workbook groups meet regularly over the course of four to six months, although it is common for some to take more time than that to complete all Twelve Steps.

Who

If you're already part of a Catholic in Recovery fellowship, either in your community or online, you might want to invite others in your meeting to be part of your small workbook group. Provide adequate notice prior to the first meeting and think about how large you want the group to be. We suggest starting with a group of between five and twelve people and closing the group when it reaches a certain capacity or after the first three small group meetings. Be clear about the time commitment and required willingness to complete the workbook at a reasonable pace.

Where

Small workbook groups gather in person or online using video conference software. It's up to you to choose the forum that works best for you. Each has its advantages and disadvantages, but the format of the meeting will remain similar whether in a virtual or in-person setting. If meeting in person, you could partner with a local church to find space to use or rely on space provided by you or another group member. Privacy and anonymity of your group members ought to be strongly valued when discerning a location.

When

If you participate in a weekly CIR meeting, it might be most appropriate to host your small workbook group before or after that meeting. The pace at which each member of the small group will work through the workbook will vary, and we suggest meeting as a small workbook group either weekly or at least every-other week. Each meeting does not have to constitute a new session if most members of the group need more time to complete the current exercise, which is most likely to occur when completing the Consequences Inventory (Step 1), the Fourth Step Inventories (Resentments, Fear, and Sex/Finance), and the process of making amends (Steps 8 and 9). Get input from the group about how to pace your progress through the workbook, but don't allow the group to rationalize dragging their feet too much!

Why

Your personal ambitions for facilitating a small workbook group should be considered and written down in some capacity. If/when you get tempted to avoid the work or prioritize other things, it will be helpful to return to your *why* in order to recommit yourself through the process. If you don't have a *why* yet, you'll find plenty upon completing your Consequences Inventory, List of *Yets*, and Vision of Hope Inventory.

Once you've found the inspiration to begin a small workbook group, established a start date, gathered members, and determined a recurring date, time, and location, be prepared to dive into the workbook material just as each of the other members of your group will. As the facilitator, you are not exempt from exploring, reflecting, and acting upon the themes of each section. In fact, your commitment to the work will set the tone for the other members' commitment.

Here is the suggested format for structuring an hour-long small workbook group session:

- Opening prayer and member introductions (3 mins)
- Group members check in and share work since last meeting (20 mins)
- Read through the next workbook section together (10 mins)

- Silently meditate on reflection questions (5 mins)
- Group sharing on reflection questions (10–15 mins)
- Introduce this week's *Putting the Steps into Action* (5–10 mins)
- Closing prayer (2 mins)

Opening Prayer and Member Introductions

At the designated start time, begin the meeting with a prayer of your choice, or invite another member to lead the group in prayer. The Serenity Prayer (found on page 173) is a good option if you're unsure what to pray. Then, invite members to introduce themselves in a way they're comfortable, beginning with yourself to provide an example. You may need to let members know that this is just an introduction—there will be plenty of time for personal sharing later in the meeting.

Group Members Check In and Share Work Since Last Meeting

This is an opportunity for each group member to briefly report anything related to their recovery that has happened over the past week and relate it to the work that has been completed since the last meeting. On your first meeting, this is where group members will each take 3–5 minutes to share their experience with addiction recovery and their personal motivations for joining the group. As the group continues to meet, this is a very important part of the meeting where members share the work from last week's *Putting the Steps into Action* or present items such as their First Step inventories (Consequences Inventory, List of Yets, and Vision of Hope), which tend to take a bit longer if done thoroughly. Make it clear to group members that this time will be a priority each week. Some group members will use this time to ask questions about concepts they don't fully understand.

Read Through the Next Workbook Section Together

Take turns reading each part of this week's workbook section. If starting a new step, read the paragraph related to the theme of the step. Then, read the section header (usually a quote), the Exploration and Understanding content, and the recovery tool(s). If a group member has a comment to make or question to ask while reading through the material, it is appropriate to pause and discuss the thought as a group. Transition to silent meditation on the reflection questions by reading the reflection questions aloud to the group.

Silently Meditate on Reflection Questions

After the reflection questions have been read, give the group five minutes of silence to quietly meditate on their own. Do the same so that you can engage in the upcoming discussion with your own experience, strength, and hope. It's recommended that you set a timer to ensure proper time.

Group Sharing on Reflection Questions

Go around the room and give each member 1–2 minutes to share their reflection on one of the questions that stood out most to them. This is a valuable part of the meeting as it offers group members a chance to gain insight on the topic from other participants before approaching the work on their own.

Introduce This Week's *Putting the Steps into Action*

Take a moment to look through the upcoming exercises, worksheets, or activities for the week ahead. Feel free to invite any initial questions that group members have, and allow others to share experience around doing similar work. It's not your job to be the expert in every facet of the Twelve Steps, and you will be able to rely on the shared hope and experience of others in the group to provide support and clarification.

Closing Prayer

Conclude the meeting by praying the prayer at the end of the section together as a group.

As with all recovery gatherings, it's important to allow time before and after the meeting for group members to connect with each other and form fellowship that extends beyond the weekly meeting. Be certain to share the responsibilities of facilitating with other group members, perhaps inviting another person to be your co-facilitator in case you are unable to make it to a meeting.

Group leader resources and additional support for facilitating a small workbook group can be accessed on the Catholic in Recovery digital platform. Visit www.catholicinrecovery.com/cirworkbook to explore more.

Catholic in Recovery (CIR) is a community of men and women finding freedom from a variety of addictions, compulsions, and unhealthy attachments. CIR offers support for individuals and families through virtual and in-person recovery meetings, retreats, online/digital resources, and content overlapping 12-step recovery principles with Catholic traditions. CIR won the top prize in the OSV Institute for Catholic Innovation Challenge Showcase in 2021.

catholicinrecovery.com
Instagram: @catholicinrecovery
Facebook: catholicinrecovery
YouTube: Catholic in Recovery

Scott Weeman is a marriage and family therapist and the founder and executive director of Catholic in Recovery, a nonprofit organization that serves individuals and families impacted by addiction. He is the author of *The Twelve Steps and the Sacraments*.

Weeman's Catholic in Recovery organization won the top prize in the OSV Institute for Catholic Innovation Challenge Showcase in 2021.

He received a bachelor's degree in organizational management from Point Loma Nazarene University, where he also earned his master's degree in clinical counseling. He has appeared on EWTN's *The Journey Home* and *Women of Grace* and is a regular guest on *Catholic Answers Live*. His work has been featured on *Aleteia* and *Patheos*.

He lives in San Diego, California, with his family.

catholicinrecovery.com
Instagram: @scottweeman
Facebook: scottweeman51
Twitter: Scott_Weeman

Further Reading for Catholics in Recovery and Those Moving toward It

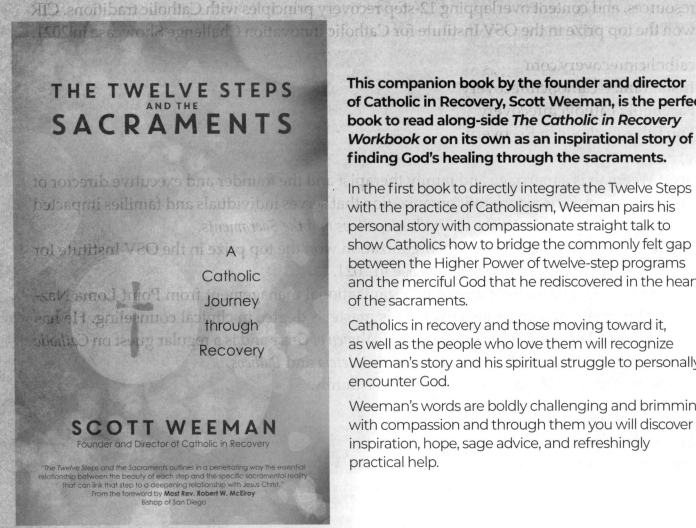

THE TWELVE STEPS
AND THE
SACRAMENTS

A
Catholic
Journey
through
Recovery

SCOTT WEEMAN
Founder and Director of Catholic in Recovery

"The Twelve Steps and the Sacraments outlines in a penetrating way the essential relationship between the beauty of each step and the specific sacramental reality that can link that step to a deepening relationship with Jesus Christ."
From the foreword by **Most Rev. Robert W. McElroy**
Bishop of San Diego

This companion book by the founder and director of Catholic in Recovery, Scott Weeman, is the perfect book to read along-side *The Catholic in Recovery Workbook* or on its own as an inspirational story of finding God's healing through the sacraments.

In the first book to directly integrate the Twelve Steps with the practice of Catholicism, Weeman pairs his personal story with compassionate straight talk to show Catholics how to bridge the commonly felt gap between the Higher Power of twelve-step programs and the merciful God that he rediscovered in the heart of the sacraments.

Catholics in recovery and those moving toward it, as well as the people who love them will recognize Weeman's story and his spiritual struggle to personally encounter God.

Weeman's words are boldly challenging and brimming with compassion and through them you will discover inspiration, hope, sage advice, and refreshingly practical help.

"In this important book, Scott Weeman shows us that the sacraments and Twelve-Step programs are complementary and that an effective recovery strategy will incorporate both."

—Jennifer Fulwiler
Bestselling author of *Something Other Than God*